A gift for

_____

From

_____

Date

_____

AN UNTROUBLED HEART

CALMING ANXIETY AND FINDING GOD'S PEACE

A 30-DAY
MORNING AND EVENING DEVOTIONAL

KARA STOUT

ZONDERVAN

An Untroubled Heart

© 2025 Kara Stout

Published in Grand Rapids, Michigan, by Zondervan. Zondervan is a registered trademark of The Zondervan Corporation, L.L.C., a wholly owned subsidary of HarperCollins Christian Publishing, Inc.

Requests for information should be addressed to customercare@harpercollins.com.

ISBN 978-0-3104-6535-5(HC)
ISBN 978-0-3104-6536-2 (audiobook)
ISBN 978-0-3104-6505-8 (eBook)

Published in association with The Bindery Agency, www.TheBinderyAgency.com.

Interior design: Kristen Sasamoto

Printed in Malaysia
25 26 27 28 29 OFF 10 9 8 7 6 5 4 3 2 1

To the one who made me a mother, my
precious daughter, Norah. I wrote
this throughout your first year of life,
writing while learning to be a mama
to you. I pray that one day you will
read this devotional, knowing it is God
who will keep your heart untroubled
throughout the ups and downs of life.
Cling to Him always, my little light.

Contents

Encouragement and a Prayer as You Begin.. ix

DAY 1   *Morning*   An Untroubled Heart.. 1
            Evening   Finding Rest for Your Soul 4

DAY 2   *Morning*   Meeting God in Your Vulnerability 7
            Evening   The Tenderness of the Lord 10

DAY 3   *Morning*   Your Soul's Signal for Help 14
            Evening   Help Comes from the Maker of Heaven
                   and Earth 17

DAY 4   *Morning*   Seeking Over Scrolling.................................... 20
            Evening   Drawing Near in the Night 23

DAY 5   *Morning*   From the Rising of the Sun to Its Setting.................... 26
            Evening   Praise Him, Moon and Stars........................... 29

DAY 6   *Morning*   The Guidance of God.................................... 32
            Evening   A Lamp to My Feet.................................... 35

DAY 7   *Morning*   Morning Glory.. 39
            Evening   Moonflowers.. 42

DAY 8   *Morning*   The One Who Daily Bears Our Burdens 45
            Evening   A Bruised Reed He Will Not Break........................... 48

DAY 9   *Morning*   When Prayers Are Not Answered in the Way
We Had Hoped 52

          Evening   The Gift of Prayer 55

DAY 10   *Morning*   The Lifter of Your Head 59

          Evening   The Strength of Your Heart 62

DAY 11   *Morning*   The Music of Morning 66

          Evening   The Symphony of Faith 69

DAY 12   *Morning*   The Steadfast Love of the Lord 73

          Evening   Recounting His Faithfulness Like Counting Stars 76

DAY 13   *Morning*   When Everything Feels Out of Control 79

          Evening   Ten Thousand Things 82

DAY 14   *Morning*   When the Cares of Your Heart Are Many 86

          Evening   The God Who Cares for You 89

DAY 15   *Morning*   Tending to Your Tears 92

          Evening   Releasing and Receiving 95

DAY 16   *Morning*   He Heals the Brokenhearted 99

          Evening   He Determines the Number of Stars 102

DAY 17   *Morning*   When I Awake, You Are Still with Me 105

          Evening   One Thing I Have Desired 108

DAY 18   *Morning*   In the Waiting 111

          Evening   I Would Have Lost Heart 114

DAY 19   *Morning*   Freedom from the Pressure to Perform 117

          Evening   God's Beautiful Poem 120

DAY 20   *Morning*   Birds of the Air 124

          Evening   Not Forgotten 127

DAY 21 *Morning* Jesu Juva 130

       Evening Soli Deo Gloria 132

DAY 22 *Morning* Trusting the One Who Calms the Storm 136

       Evening A Mind Stayed on God 139

DAY 23 *Morning* A Rhythm of Prayer 143

       Evening A Rhythm of Repentance 146

DAY 24 *Morning* Morning Light 149

       Evening Tucked in God's Grace 152

DAY 25 *Morning* Not Alone 156

       Evening Your Comforting Companion 159

DAY 26 *Morning* Stopping to Smell the Roses 162

       Evening Resting in Gratitude 165

DAY 27 *Morning* Where Morning Dawns 169

       Evening Where Evening Fades 172

DAY 28 *Morning* A Heart Like a Garden 176

       Evening To Know Him Is to Love Him 179

DAY 29 *Morning* The Lord Is My Shepherd 183

       Evening Under His Wings 186

DAY 30 *Morning* The Scent of Heaven 190

       Evening Shalom, Peace 193

Notes 197

About the Author 198

Encouragement and a Prayer as You Begin

Y ou're so strong."
I remember hearing this repeatedly from friends and family as I walked through difficult experiences in my life: recovering from a carotid artery dissection, struggling with infertility, facing financial hardship, caring for my mother through her cancer journey, and losing her after having already lost my dad.

But no matter what it may have looked like on the outside, I felt completely weak. My troubles weighed on my heart, my trust in God was tested, and my peace was shaken. I felt overwhelmed and anxious. In the morning, a rush of to-dos, pressure, and thoughts flooded my mind upon waking. At night, I felt the weight of everything I was carrying and would lie down feeling drained and tearful. Maybe you've felt the same?

The troubles weighed on my heart, yet what God taught me (and what He is continuing to teach me) in these seasons was how to calm anxiety and find His peace in all circumstances. He showed me it was possible to keep my heart untroubled by learning how to let my peace rest on Jesus alone. And that is what I want to share with you here in these pages.

Right now may be a time in your life that feels incredibly hard and overwhelming. You may have tried to hold on to peace, but circumstances and trials have made it difficult. Or maybe you have become so used to anxiety that you are accustomed to its presence. But oh, friend, there is a remedy for the troubles of your heart.

This morning and evening devotional is designed as a twice-daily reminder that God is the remedy. Each day sets the intention to begin and end in a place of renewed hope and strength, stillness and trust, refreshed and reminded of God's goodness and faithfulness.

My hope is that this thirty-day journey will help you draw near to God as the sun rises and again when the day draws to a close, giving you an opportunity to go to Him and release all the worries, tears, and fears you're holding in. As you read and pray each morning and night, may you feel His nearness, comfort, and peace so that you can rest, *truly rest*, in His steadfast love.

I'm so grateful to be spending time with you these next thirty days and that you have chosen this devotional as a morning and evening companion to lead you to your Greatest Companion, the only One who can keep your heart untroubled. He hasn't left you. You have not been forgotten by God. As His

Word reminds us in Acts 17, "He is actually not far from each one of us, for 'In him we live and move and have our being'" (27–28).

My Prayer for You As You Begin This Devotional

Heavenly Father,

I pray for Your daughter who is holding this book in her hands, who is deeply desiring Your nearness, whose heart needs You. She is weary and she is coming to You.

I pray she would feel Your embrace, Your tenderness and strength. I pray her worries and anxiety would dissolve as she spends time in Your presence and gentle grace—that she would experience true peace that brings rest to her soul.

May she be given courage and joy to face each new day, and may she be given a renewed understanding of her value and how much You love her. I pray she would learn more about Your character—and not just know about You but know You more personally and intimately.

I pray she would grow deeper in her faith and that her relationship with Jesus would become even sweeter. I pray the Holy Spirit would bring comfort and healing to the parts of her heart that are burdened or broken.

May she be reminded of Your steadfast love every morning and be tucked in Your grace every night as she journeys through this book. In Jesus' name I pray, amen.

"Let not your heart be troubled, neither let it be afraid."

John 14:27 NKJV

An Untroubled Heart

"Peace I leave with you; my peace I give you. I do
not give to you as the world gives. Do not let your
hearts be troubled and do not be afraid."

JOHN 14:27 NIV

Morning

R ight now your heart may be troubled and burdened with
worries. My prayer is for God to bring relief and peace to
your heart in this moment and as we walk through these thirty
days together.

The well-being of your heart matters to Jesus. When the
Bible talks about "the heart," it is referring to the very core of
who we are. An article I read explains this further: "The Bible
mentions the heart almost 1,000 times. In essence, this is what
it says: the heart is that spiritual part of us where our emotions
and desires dwell."[1]

Twice in John 14, Jesus said to "not let your hearts be
troubled" (vv. 1, 27 NIV). These words He spoke to His disciples
are encouragement for us today as Christians on a journey
through an anxiety-ridden world of brokenness, hardships,
and worries. His words reassure us that it is possible to have
untroubled hearts in this life, in these circumstances, in the
middle of trials and uncertain outcomes.

Jesus promised His peace, a peace radically different from the peace the world gives. The peace of this world is fleeting, unreliable, and deceptive, and it ultimately leaves us empty. The peace of Jesus is lasting, dependable, true, and satisfying. We can trust the words of Jesus. We can stop and breathe. We can be overwhelmed not with worry but with divine peace. We can exchange a troubled heart for an untroubled heart.

Lord,

I pray for an untroubled heart: a heart that is not easily disturbed or worried, one that resides in Your peace and makes its home under Your wings. Only You, and You alone, can speak to my heart, making me feel safe and calm. I have succumbed to the cycle of anxiety, but in this moment I ask You to break this cycle and any learned habits or tendencies of anxiety.

I surrender to the truth that Your peace is attainable in this world. Not because of perfect circumstances or a life without stress or hardships but because You give us Your peace. Because You—the One who created my heart, my very being—bring me the deepest peace, the peace that surpasses all understanding.

Would You show me if there are things of this world I trust for peace more than You? Help me to no longer trust in this false peace but in You, my true peace.

As I begin this journey over the next thirty days, I ask that You would transform me by the power of Your Spirit to be someone who carries Your peace daily throughout all circumstances. I pray to continually seek You as my peace, to trust in Your care, and to remember that despite the troubles of this world and this life, I can have an untroubled heart in You. In Jesus' name I pray, amen.

Finding Rest for Your Soul

"Come to me, all you who are weary and burdened,
and I will give you rest. Take my yoke upon you and
learn from me, for I am gentle and humble in heart,
and you will find rest for your souls."

MATTHEW 11:28–29 NIV

Evening

Not too long ago I read these familiar verses in Matthew. Three words kept repeating in my spirit: "Come to me." Had I become so familiar with these verses that I missed the actual call to stop being distracted and go to Jesus? It was both convicting and healing in that it was clear that my weariness had a remedy, a solution found only in time spent with Jesus.

Sometimes we read these words and unknowingly miss an important part of what Jesus is saying. We see the promise of rest but don't see our part in this exchange. There is a necessary response to His call, an intentional action. We cannot read this offer from Jesus and think that just reading it will provide rest.

If we are often weary and tired and longing for rest, it may be because we neglect to come to Jesus. When we hear His invitation, we must move toward Him. We must go to our Savior who is waiting for us to come to Him. Within time together lies the uncovered treasure of true, deep, transformative, abiding rest.

The rest we yearn for comes in stillness, prayer, worship, reading God's Word, time spent in nature, and other ways Jesus knows are personally restful for you. Rest can come even in the busiest of days. When we abide in Him continually, we have His rest available continually. Augustine of Hippo summarized this promise of finding rest in Christ so sweetly and succinctly when he wrote, "You have made us for yourself, and our heart is restless until it rests in you."[2]

If your heart has been heavy and burdened, weary and troubled, Jesus sees you and is calling you to come to Him. An untroubled heart is a heart at rest, content in Christ. I pray this devotional will help you build a practice of coming to Jesus morning and evening, for with Him you will find your greatest rest, your steadfast contentment, your untroubled heart.

Jesus,

My heart has been heavy and burdened, weary and needing rest. But I know You are calling to me, calling for me to come spend time with You and receive Your gift of rest.

My soul is attentive to Your words. I hear Your invitation, one that is so sweet to my ears: "Come to me." So I come, kneeling at Your feet, and rest. I come, embracing You, and rest. I come to dwell with You—and rest.

And I recognize yet again that I am content only in You. My soul is at rest only in You. My act of rest proclaims my trust in You, and I do, Lord—I trust in You. And I love You. Amen.

Meeting God in Your Vulnerability

> I prayed to the LORD, and he answered me. He
> freed me from all my fears. Those who look to him
> for help will be radiant with joy; no shadow of
> shame will darken their faces.
>
> PSALM 34:4–5 NLT

————— *Morning* —————

The human experience is layered with emotions that can draw us near to God. Part of being human is experiencing emotions like worry, fear, sadness, and anxiety at times. Given the brokenness of this world and life's difficulties, uncertainties, trauma, and pain, it's impossible to escape such emotions.

It is the God we turn to in our painful emotions that makes all the difference. Emotions tell us of our need for God. Because how would we know we needed God's help, strength, comfort, protection, peace, and rest if we didn't first experience an emotion that told us we needed those very things? When we experience worry, we realize we need God's peace; when we experience fear, we need God's help; when we experience despair, we need God's comfort; and so on. In this world we will have troubles (John 16:33). And we lean on God when troubles come, when worries come, when fears come. We shouldn't try to bypass these emotions, or we run the great risk of missing out on an abiding, deep relationship with our Father.

Instead of looking to God for help, we may attempt self-reliance. We may try to pacify our worries quickly on our own or try to numb them. But we don't want to fall into the trap of robotically pushing past our emotions, because our emotions should lead us *to* God. Our human experience is the framework for our relationship with God, and the emotions we experience can lead to a growing intimacy and a *real* knowing of Him. If we stuff our feelings down or try to handle them in our own strength, our mental, physical, and spiritual health are at stake, as well as a genuine relationship with God.

In this morning's verses from Psalms, we see that the key is to "look to Him for help" when we experience painful emotions. The psalmist, David, was experiencing fear, and by looking to God, he was freed from all his fears. Not only that, but he told us we will be radiant with joy when we look to God for help. What a contrast—from fear to radiant with joy! Only God can do that. Notice also how David wrote, "No shadow of shame will darken their faces." Shame that comes from experiencing anxiety and fear can place us in bondage right along with the anxiety and fear. If we try to hide our worries instead of going to God, that can steal the very freedom we are seeking. There is no shame, ever, in needing God and seeking His help.

Allow your emotions to bring you truthfully and vulnerably to your Father. Embrace the intimacy that comes when you go to a holy, kind, and sovereign God to free you from all your fears, a God who shows compassion toward you in those moments, not condemnation.

O Lord,

I am comforted this morning knowing that You walk with me in my human experience. You are already aware of what I am going through. You are already aware of my emotions. You know them and see them because You made me and know me.

Freedom from all my fears is found in You. You hear when I call to You; You do not turn Your face away when I experience emotions because of life's difficulties and pain.

Please guard me from the lie that I can handle my fears and worries in my own strength. Please guard me from suppressing or bypassing my emotions. I trust in You, not myself, to relieve my worries.

When I look away from my fears and to You, I am radiant with joy! How I see Your glory and give You all the glory, my loving Lord. Amen.

The Tenderness of the Lord

As a father shows compassion to his children, so the
LORD shows compassion to those who fear him. For
he knows our frame; he remembers that we are dust.

PSALM 103:13–14

Evening

When I was twenty-nine, exactly one month after I got married, I had a carotid artery dissection. This is when a tear occurs in one of your carotid arteries, which can compromise blood flow to the brain and lead to a stroke. Yes, this is extremely rare, especially at a young age. I had all the symptoms of a stroke, but praise God, I did not actually have one. I had what is called a transient ischemic attack (TIA), which presented as numbness and tingling on one side of my body, loss of vision in one eye, and difficulty with speech, all of which resolved and didn't cause long-term damage, thankfully! I was monitored in the hospital for five days. I didn't need surgery but was on blood thinners for several months as my artery healed.

Surprisingly, I was not afraid or worried during the actual event, or even while I was in the hospital. I felt blanketed by His peace and protection. At one point I was so weak, I was barely able to walk to the bathroom while hooked up to my IV. In that moment I saw a vision of Jesus holding me up and walking with me. It was as though I could physically feel His tenderness, sympathy, and compassion carrying me.

Afterward, when I came home from the hospital, I began to feel fearful and worried a TIA would happen again, or even a stroke. I also worried about work and how I would perform, feeling the way that I did. God saw my anxieties and fears and moved toward me in tenderness. As I came to Him in prayer, my anxieties and fears diminished. In continually going to God, the intensity, frequency, and duration of my worries and anxieties lessened and lessened.

The Lord met me in this experience with tenderness. I discovered His compassion and care, both at the initial moment of crisis and in the days following when I felt fearful. He knew my physical weakness as well as my emotional and mental weakness. He was my Father, showing me compassion. When I had imaging done again ten years later, my artery was completely healed, as if the dissection never happened. It "looked beautiful" according to my doctor!

Can you think of a time when you saw the tenderness of Jesus carrying and sustaining you? I pray that as you recall this time, you would fall asleep tonight remembering that His tenderness remains. In all of life's experiences, He will continue to hold you up, friend. In your worries and fears, in your human frame, Christ holds you up.

My Lord,

How calming it is for my soul tonight to consider Your compassion, to recall Your kindness and care. Your tenderness has healed me time and time again. I pray that my gratitude for Your lovingkindness will rise up to You like incense.

You are a compassionate God, One who displays sympathy, One who moves toward us in our need for You. Your tenderness meets me in my vulnerability. It holds me up in this season, and I know it will continue to hold me up in every season for the remainder of my life. Amen.

God is our refuge and strength, an
ever-present help in trouble.

Psalm 46:1 NIV

Your Soul's Signal for Help

From the end of the earth I will cry to You, when my heart is overwhelmed; lead me to the rock that is higher than I.

PSALM 61:2 NKJV

Morning

A signal tells us that something needs attending to. It conveys critical information, and it is not something to ignore. It is wise to be attentive to signals so we will know what to do when they occur. Consider a car. A car is built with warning lights that alert us when things need attention. And we rely on the mechanic for help to fix the issue. If we didn't have a signal, we wouldn't realize we needed help. How imperative a signal is!

Anxiety is one of your soul's signals for help, a signal that your soul needs tending to. Instead of succumbing to anxious thoughts or feeling captive to anxiety, what if we recognized anxiety as a signal alerting us to go to God? What if we saw it as a reminder to quickly go to Him for help because He loves us? Instead of surrendering to worries, we surrender to our sovereign God. And in doing so, we stop the recycling of our anxious thoughts, recognizing our need for God and praying for His help.

This morning's scripture paints an intimate, honest picture of David crying out to God, knowing his refuge and peace could be found only in Him. He sensed his heart was overwhelmed, he acknowledged this signal, and he called out to God. He recognized his need for God, his need for God's help. And he prayed, "Lead me to the rock that is higher than I."

When we allow the signal alert of anxiety to go unchecked for too long without going to the Father, we can become drained or sick with worry. If this is where you find yourself right now, I want to remind you that the Lord is near. He has not left you on your own to deal with life's worries and hardships. God cares for you and cares when your heart is troubled. He will help you with the worries and troubles you've been carrying for too long.

We must not overlook this signal of the soul. We must not allow it to linger and become too familiar and thus not as quickly attended to. Pay attention to your soul's signals, consider what they are telling you, and keep leaning on the God of comfort and compassion for help.

Father,
Help me see my painful emotions as opportunities to come to You, as signals that alert me to my deep need for

You. Signals that tell me I am hurting, overwhelmed, and not okay. Signals that lead me to You, my Maker, for help, consolation, and healing. Signals that remind me restorative relief and strength are found in You.

Teach me to quickly recognize when my soul is signaling for help. Let me not delay in coming to You. I know I cannot fight anxiety and worry in my own strength, and I don't want to. I come to You to lift off my anxiety; I come to You for strength and peace. I come to You. Amen.

Help Comes from the Maker of Heaven and Earth

I lift up my eyes to the hills. From where does my help come? My help comes from the LORD, who made heaven and earth.

PSALM 121:1–2

Evening

God—who created the heavens and the earth, the sky and clouds, the moon and stars, the oceans and all that's in them, the mountains and trees, every flower, every petal, every single creature, you and me—is our Helper. How astonishing is this thought! When we truly pause to think about it, it's incredibly and deeply comforting.

When you need help, where do you go? Do you go to God first? He tells us in His Word that He is our help. If we know He is the Lord who made heaven and earth, why do we ever hesitate or forget to go to Him for help? Why are we sometimes slow to go to Him, oftentimes trying first on our own to solve our problems, to comfort ourselves, to fix our worries, to control our circumstances?

How great and constant is our need for our Helper! Our daily language must include asking and reaching for Him continuously for help. Because what greater help is there on earth or in heaven than the help from the One who created it all? Our majestic, powerful, and kind God sees and responds to our reaching for Him. He moves toward us, and He helps us.

The Maker of heaven and earth is also the Maker of every human. God has created us to be there for one another, to receive help and to give help. This truth is a wonderful reminder that we also receive His help through the help and love of others in the form of friends, family, community, therapists, and even strangers sometimes. Let Him guide you to the help He knows is best for your soul.

Today's verses are from the Psalms, a beautiful book in the Bible layered with moments of desperate need for God and God's response, His nearness, His concern, His help. And it's not just in the book of Psalms that we see evidence of God as our Helper. It is woven throughout the entirety of Scripture. Read these additional verses tonight to remind your soul that God is your help:

Psalm 46:1
Psalm 54:4
Psalm 63:7
Psalm 124:8
John 14:16–17
Hebrews 13:6

Lord,

You are my ever-present help. Oh, that I would not forget this promise or ever take it for granted! I know Your help; I have experienced it time and time again, when I have cried out or prayed a simple prayer.

My heart stirs within me as I consider that You, the Maker of heaven and earth, also call Yourself my Helper. You have not let Your creation fend for itself. You have not created us and then left us to be without the help of our Creator. How wonderful are Your ways, how kind is Your heart.

May I seek Your help often and quickly. Keep me from self-reliance and from allowing myself to get overwhelmed rather than first praying, "Lord, help me."

I love You and am so thankful that You, Lord, are my Maker and my Helper. In Jesus' name I pray, amen.

Seeking Over Scrolling

And without faith it is impossible to please him, for
whoever would draw near to God must believe that
he exists and that he rewards those who seek him.

HEBREWS 11:6

Morning

Several years ago I became increasingly aware of what social
media was doing to my soul, my time, and my relationship
with God. The more time I spent on social media, the more I
was drained, discontent, and distracted. I felt convicted and
encouraged by the Holy Spirit to make some necessary and
healthy changes that would be restorative to my soul.

I began to leave my phone on the dining room table at
night, not bringing it into my bedroom. That way I'd no longer
be tempted to spend time on it in bed before falling asleep,
and it wouldn't be the first thing I grabbed upon waking. I
also started a weekly phone sabbath of putting my phone in a
drawer every Friday evening and not pulling it out again until
Sunday morning. Implementing this weekly practice brought
refreshment every weekend. These developed into habits that
continue to this day, and it's made all the difference in my life.

These regular breaks from my phone continue to help me
gain greater peace and a healthier perspective on social media.

I have found it truly beneficial for my soul, my faith, my marriage, and my parenting. Setting intentional time away from my phone has been a life-changing, needed practice, one I recommend trying if you haven't already.

There is an impact on your spirit when you feed your heart with a flood of content right before bed and then again upon waking. When we begin and end our days on our phones, we start scrolling, lose track of time, and find ourselves left with an empty, discontent feeling. We may begin to compare and analyze our lives, giving way to a false need to keep up with others, their clothing, their families, or their homes. We may feel overwhelmed by all the conflicting information or the unkind words carelessly said online, all of which can deplete us and affect us more than we fully realize or understand. We may end up putting our phones down feeling sad, anxious, agitated, or jealous.

This is the opposite of how we feel when we sit before the Lord and draw near to Him. Take notice of the contrast between your time spent on social media and the peaceful, still waters the Lord leads you along. This nothing-else-in-the-world-like-it peace is profoundly different from any feelings found in mindlessly scrolling.

Social media can certainly be used for good. But when the balance tips to becoming unhealthy for our minds, spirits, and hearts, when it hinders precious time spent with God, we need to step back, set boundaries and time limits, and work to break the unhealthy phone habits we have allowed. We should aim to have self-control over our use of social media rather than allowing it to control us.

If you're feeling anxious and drained from too much time on your phone, would you join me in seeking God over scrolling?

Lord,

Above all things I can seek, I want to seek You. I want to seek You more, and I want to seek You first. When it comes to social media, I can sometimes get lost in that world and become distracted. I ask for Your help in setting healthy boundaries, and may Your Spirit help me grow in the fruit of self-control.

Remind me to pray before opening social media, and keep me firmly rooted in You and Your peace as I navigate the social media world. I ask for forgiveness for the times I have placed spending time on my phone over time with You.

Guide my time and guard my time, Lord. Help me engage in social media in a way that is honoring to You. May it be used for good and for Your glory. In Jesus' name I pray, amen.

Drawing Near in the Night

But for me it is good to be near God; I have made
the Lord GOD my refuge, that I may tell of all your
works.

PSALM 73:28

Evening

As tonight's psalm says, "For me it is good to be near God."
Day and night, it is good for us to be near God. Drawing
near in the night is an opportunity and an invitation that we
sometimes, maybe even oftentimes, miss. Oh, that we would
embrace such nightly opportunities!

Night after night as we draw near, we are cultivating more
and more deeply our most treasured relationship with our most
treasured Delight. Scripture promises the gift of God drawing
near to us as we draw near to Him (James 4:8).

We long for peace in this world, yet do we truly take the
time to draw near to our Prince of Peace? Charles Spurgeon
defines our faith as dependent upon drawing near to Jesus,
saying in one of his sermons: "Faith in Christ is simply and
truly described as coming to him. . . . Coming is a very simple
action indeed; it seems to have only two things about it, one is,
to come *away from* something, and the other is, to come *to* something."[3] This applies not only to our initial moment of coming

to Him for our salvation but also continually coming to Him for peace, strength, comfort, and companionship.

Take an inventory of the things that you need to move away from, the actions that are distracting you from spending time with God in the evenings. Is it possibly too much TV or time on your phone or social media? Ask the Holy Spirit to reveal what is hindering you from drawing even closer to God in the evenings.

There is something so delicate and intimate about the night, those tender moments to draw close to the Father, a time to express our longings to Him, our hurts, our tears, our honesty, our vulnerability. Let us set aside distractions and draw near in stillness, in quietness, in adoration. Let Him be who you go to at the end of the day. He is truly what your heart needs, what it longs for.

Heavenly Father,

The evening greets me, and I come to You. I draw near to You in the night.

I talk with You, sharing about my day. Although You already know all that happened, You listen. I reflect on how You were with me throughout the day. And I begin to thank You, overwhelmed by Your wonderful ways, Your Fatherly love.

I bring You the things on my mind, my concerns, my hurts. I bring You my gratitude, my praise, my love. And I see so clearly that it is good to be near You.

I yearn to grow in intimacy with You, in the morning, throughout the day, and in the evening. Please help me turn off the distractions before bed and come to You. May my heart desire time with You every evening.

In Jesus' name I pray, amen.

From the Rising of the Sun to Its Setting

From the rising of the sun to its setting, the name of
the LORD is to be praised!

PSALM 113:3

Morning

There is something so beautiful about a sunrise and a
sunset to mark the beginning and ending of a day. The
brilliant colors of the sunrise, orange and red, bring praise to
the Lord for a new day that He has made. The sun itself brings
praise to God for His greatness and splendor, in how He has
created it to be precisely the ideal size, color, and distance to
support life on earth.

Each morning, I wake up Norah, our six-month-old baby
girl, by opening the drapes in her nursery. Immediately her
face lights up with a big smile as she looks outside at the new
day. And I say something along the lines of "Wow, look at what
all God has made!" Together we marvel as we look outside at
the sun, sky, clouds, and trees, her little face delighting in what
she sees.

Our intimacy with God deepens and grows when we praise
Him. Praising God means exalting Him, giving Him love and
honor and thanksgiving. We praise Him in our praying, in our

working, in our resting, in our singing. We praise Him by our thoughts, our words, our conversations, our testimonies. Praise expresses adoration for who He is: His majesty, His holiness, His mercy, His faithfulness, His grace, His forgiveness, His salvation.

Honest praise is beautiful in the sight of the Lord. We can praise Him in our joy, in our thankfulness, in our sorrow, in our laughter, in our calm, in our tears, in our trials. Praise disrupts worry and uplifts an anxious, troubled heart. Today, may we focus on praising the Lord, adoring and exalting Him from the rising of the sun to its setting.

PRAYERS OF PRAISE TO READ IN SCRIPTURE
Psalm 63:3
Psalm 71:6
Isaiah 25:1
Jeremiah 17:14

DECLARATIONS OF PRAISE TO READ IN SCRIPTURE
Psalm 66:1–4
Psalm 100:4
Psalm 104:33
Psalm 147:1

Lord,

Each sunrise is a reminder of Your steadfast love. The brilliant orange and red colors that light up the morning sky announce Your majesty and faithfulness. From the rising of the sun to its setting, I praise You, giving You an offering of praise from hour to hour.

I praise You for Your goodness, holiness, justice, mercy, grace, forgiveness, and salvation. I praise You by my thoughts, words, conversations, and testimony. I praise You in joy, in thankfulness, in sorrow, in laughter, in calm, in tears, in trials.

From birth I have relied on You; I will ever praise You (Psalm 71:6). I will praise You to my last breath (104:33)! I love You. Amen.

Praise Him, Moon and Stars

Praise him, sun and moon; praise him, all you
shining stars.

PSALM 148:3 NIV

Evening

Astronaut John Glenn, the first American to orbit the
earth, said to reporters after he had just returned from
his second and final trip to space, "To look out at this kind of
creation and not believe in God is to me impossible."[4]

Our God created the sky. He stretched out the heavens and
blanketed the night sky with billions of stars. And each one is
unique! Billions of stars and not one like the other, not a single
one (1 Corinthians 15:41). This continues in all His creation:
animals, snowflakes, trees, leaves, flowers. Not one is identical,
not one is exactly like another. It is the same with us. Billions
of people have walked this earth and not one person is exactly
like another. No wonder all of creation praises Him!

Oceans and mountains, plants and animals, the sun and
moon, every shining star, every person, all are in His hands.
We can see God's mighty works in everything. Nothing is arbi-
trary. Nothing came into being without the power of His hand;
nothing is sustained without the authority of His sovereign will.
We can see the effects of His majesty everywhere our eyes land.

And then consider what our eyes don't see: all that is at work within the entire universe and within our own bodies that He so wonderfully created. This all could not happen simply by chance. Every detail was divinely designed, created perfectly and precisely with us in mind.

Meditating on His greatness and artistry provokes our hearts to delight in His magnificence. So, tonight, let's join the moon and the stars and all of creation in praising Him!

Maker and Sustainer of all,

You are worthy to receive praise, love, and honor! For all things were created by You and exist by Your goodwill. The heavens declare Your glory; the skies proclaim the work of Your hands (Psalm 19:1).

When I look at the night sky, I know it is You who created each star. You call each one by name. How intimately You know creation, for You are the very Creator of it all.

When I consider that You, the One who created the sun and moon and every star, are mindful of me and care for me, my soul fills with the sweetest peace and gratitude. You are wonderful, and my heart praises You as I fall asleep tonight. Amen.

Lift up your eyes and look to the heavens: Who created all these? He who brings out the starry host one by one and calls forth each of them by name.

Isaiah 40:26 NIV

The Guidance of God

Let the morning bring me word of your unfailing
love, for I have put my trust in you. Show me the
way I should go, for to you I entrust my life.

PSALM 143:8 NIV

Morning

I love to pray today's verse when waking. It is an honest desire
to remember God's love for me and to trust in Him again
with whatever today brings. Knowing He will guide me and
show me the way I should go gives me courage to begin again.

Seeking God's guidance is an act of humility, an act of surrender, an act of acknowledging that He is Lord of all and all
His ways are good and right. Our relationship with Him grows
as He shows us the way we should go. As we follow, we get to
know our walking Companion more and more. As we follow, our
continual communication with Him brings peace and wisdom as
we daily look to our loving Guide.

There are certain times in life when we feel we are at a
crossroads, when we cannot see the path clearly and desperately need His guidance. When I've had big decisions to make,
I've thought, *I just wish I could sit down face-to-face with God and
ask Him what I should do.* Have you ever felt this way? When my

husband and I were praying through whether to seek fertility treatments or adoption, this was a reoccurring thought of mine. I just wanted the decision to be clear right away.

God didn't reveal His plan to us immediately, but He did make clear our next steps until we saw His perfect plan unfold. As hard as it can be to wait on the direction of the Lord, this creates an opportunity to depend on Him, step by step, day by day, decision by decision.

Throughout the Bible, there are numerous examples of God gradually guiding His people and His people learning to faithfully follow His leading and wait on His timing.

Take the life of Moses. In the book of Exodus, when God enlisted Moses to help free His people from slavery in Egypt, God didn't reveal the entire plan to him all at once. Moses had to follow where God led, act when God told him to act, and trust God was in control. Moses looked to God throughout a series of plagues, when God led His people to the banks of the Red Sea, and when they needed food and water in the desert. Each time, God showed He was trustworthy: freeing His people, parting waters, sending bread from heaven, and bringing water from a rock.

This is often how He leads us in life: in steps. We don't get an entire blueprint of what's to come. He provides just what we need to take the next step in the direction He is leading. We can be reassured He will keep us moving at His pace, as we hold His guiding hand.

Lord,

As the morning comes, I am reminded of Your unfailing love, and it gives me courage and joy to face this new day. Show me the way I should go, that I may know You more and know the path to take.

I ask for insight into Your will, that I may follow it. Sometimes when there are different ways to go, I feel uncertain and need Your clarity. I will go where You lead. You hold me by the hand as I take each step. Your presence brings peace as I walk on the path You are laying out before me.

Increase my ability to discern what doors You have opened and what doors You have closed. Bring to life the purposes for which You have created me. In Jesus' name I pray, amen.

A Lamp to My Feet

Your word is a lamp to my feet and a light
to my path.

PSALM 119:105

Evening

O ne of the greatest treasures we have been given is the
Bible. It is a lamp to our feet, illuminating the path God
is leading us on. His Word makes clear the steps to take, continually showing us the way we should go. Second Timothy
3:16 says, "All Scripture is God-breathed" (NIV). The Bible is
His precious Word to us so that we can know Him, learn from
Him, and be transformed and guided by Him.

His Word guides us in every facet of life. It was written
for our instruction and encouragement (Romans 15:4) as we
journey through this world. We read the Bible to gain insight,
wisdom, and guidance to help us make daily decisions that are
aligned with God's will. And we look to Jesus' teachings docu-
mented in the Gospels to lead us and steady us on the path
of God.

We are students of His Word all our lives, so we make it a
priority to spend time within its life-giving, life-leading pages.
We must study and know the Word of God for ourselves, carrying our lamp close so we won't wander in the darkness. Scripture

anchors us in God's truth so we aren't tossed around by worldly temptations or false ways. It is a light to our path, protecting us from being deceived.

Oh, that His Word would be engraved on our hearts, that we would know it and live by it, that we would "be doers of the word, and not hearers only" (James 1:22)! We read in Matthew 4:4, "Man shall not live by bread alone, but by every word that comes from the mouth of God." Do we live on the Word of God as we live on food? His Word sustains us, nourishes us, renews us. As His child, you are meant to live by the radiant lamp of His Word that guides your footsteps day by day.

When we make reading Scripture an intentional habit, we make a habit of centering our minds and our hearts on His truth and His path. Our days and our lives are beautifully and significantly impacted by His Word. Peace comes to the anxious heart, wisdom to the seeking soul, guidance to the humble follower, joy to the child of God, strength to the weary.

May you fall asleep tonight knowing God has lovingly given you His Spirit and His Word to guide you.

Thank You, God, for Your Word.

May I never take it for granted, may I cherish it always, for it is more precious than gold. The more time I spend in Your Word, the more I get to know You, and You are wonderful.

Your Word guides me, making clear the path. "Direct my footsteps according to your word" (Psalm 119:133 NIV), and engrave it upon my heart, that I would live a life that is pleasing to You. In Jesus' name I pray, amen.

Shout for joy to God, all the earth; sing the glory
of his name; give to him glorious praise!

Psalm 66:1–2

Morning Glory

"You are worthy, our Lord and God, to receive glory and honor and power, for you created all things, and by your will they were created and have their being."

REVELATION 4:11 NIV

Morning

When my husband and I first moved to California, I noticed beautiful flowers on vines growing along walls and gates and up trees. The name of this flower is simply perfect: morning glory. Typically, these flowers unfold into full bloom in the early morning. Most of the ones I see are a deep purple color, and when you look close, they shimmer. The center even appears as if it's glowing. The tiny specks of glitter within the petals always bring joyous praise to my heart.

These perfectly named flowers proclaim the glory of God as the day begins. This flowering vine has become a picture to me of how I want to give glory to God. As the sun comes up, I want His glory to be first on my mind.

His magnificence and power are made known in every sunrise, in every flower. Their beauty speaks to His beauty. Everything points with overwhelming evidence to the truth that He is glorious and wonderful and worthy of all our love and devotion. When we consider our amazing Creator, the ultimate Artist, and His billions of creations, all varied and unique, His glory cannot be denied.

Deeply enjoying the wonders of His works brings us a sense of calm and joy. We often get so busy that we miss it—we miss His glory that surrounds us each day. Delighting in God and His creativity sets our hearts on Him and puts them at rest. I want to pay attention to His glory in His creation every day. I pray that I, too, would be one of His creations that points to His glory, that I would awake to reflect His glory, that I would live not for my own glory but for His.

We give Him glory by abiding in Christ, who is the True Vine (John 15:1–17). Dwelling and delighting in Christ brings praise to the Father and a sweet tranquility as we begin the day. May we be like morning glory flowers, abiding in the vine, reflecting the beauty of our Creator and proclaiming His glory.

Father,

I sit in awe of You this morning, in awe of Your crea-tions. Your eternal power and divine nature are so evident and have been since the creation of the world (Romans 1:20).

Open my eyes to see, really see, Your artwork on display.

All of creation tells of Your majesty, Your Artist's hand upon it all. Thousands upon thousands of Your creations—how can I not see You in everything? Every creation is a reflection of Your glory, Your wonder, Your beauty, Your love.

Sometimes I fall for the lie that I'm too busy to stop, look up, and look around. Help me this morning to take special notice of one or two of Your creations: a flower, a tree, the sunshine, the rain, a bird singing, a body of water, clouds.

Help me depend on Jesus, my Vine, to be like that of a morning glory, to declare Your glory and reflect Your glory today and every day. Amen.

Moonflowers

"In the same way, let your light shine before
others, so that they may see your good works
and give glory to your Father who is in heaven."

MATTHEW 5:16

Evening

H ave you ever heard of moonflowers? I recently learned about them. They are a species of morning glory. These nocturnal plants fascinate me and beautifully demonstrate our purpose in Christ.

Moonflowers are given their name because they bloom at night and close during the daytime. Typically, these flowers are an iridescent white with a sweet aroma emanating from them, lovely to behold. Morning glories open as the sun begins to rise while moonflowers open as the sun goes down. Both have their own beauty, both have their own purpose, both bloom according to God's timing, and both bloom to show the glory of God.

When researching moonflowers, I read, "When the sun sets, they open up to an astounding six or seven inch long bloom."[5] This led me to consider: In the darkness, do I open to my greatest bloom, giving glory to God in the night? Or do I stay closed in the darkness? I thought of Jesus' words encouraging and commissioning us to be the light of the world and to let our lights shine for the glory of the Father (Matthew 5:14–16). We receive our light from Jesus, as He is *the* Light of the world, and in Him we radiate His light. As the moon stands out against a night sky, as your eye cannot help but be drawn to the moon reflecting the light of the sun, so we are to be like moonflowers blooming in the darkness.

This comparison to moonflowers also reminds me of Jeremiah 17:7–8: "Blessed is the one who trusts in the LORD, whose confidence is in him. They will be like a tree planted by the water that sends out its roots by the stream. It does not fear when heat comes; its leaves are always green. It has no worries in a year of drought and never fails to bear fruit" (NIV). The tree doesn't fear heat or drought because its roots draw water from the source. In a similar fashion, when we turn to Jesus as the source of our light, we bloom like flowers who do not fear when the night comes.

Friend, remember, it is when our faith remains planted firmly in Him that we bloom, despite the weather and seasons, day or night. God created us to stand out in the darkness; He created us to be rooted in His grace and His love; He created us to release the fragrance of Christ (2 Corinthians 2:15). Like moonflowers, we, too, have our ordained purpose of blooming in the darkness, not fearing when the night comes but bringing the light of Christ to all we encounter.

Lord,

Thank You for the lessons revealed in nature and the encouragement that comes as I consider the moonflower: how it opens in its ordained time, how it blooms despite the darkness, how it diffuses a sweet fragrance crafted by You, how it is dressed beautifully in white against the backdrop of darkness.

Draw me close; help me remain rooted in You. By the grace of Your hand, I am planted and nourished, growing, unfolding, and blooming to display Your light to those walking in darkness. Amen.

The One Who Daily Bears Our Burdens

Cast your burden on the LORD, and he will sustain you; he will never permit the righteous to be moved.

PSALM 55:22

Morning

I sat with my mom in the doctor's office as he confirmed her diagnosis: she had stage 4 cancer. Although God had been preparing me, the moment still didn't seem real. Her sweet head looked down to take it in as both of us tried to grasp what would lie ahead, what our next steps would be, and what this diagnosis would mean for the years we thought we would have together.

When we left the office, we sat in the car together crying. With tears in her eyes, she immediately prayed. She began by thanking God for His faithfulness in carrying her through past heartbreak and suffering, knowing He would carry her yet again. Her decision to trust the Father to sustain her was deeply impactful to witness. I saw Him pick her up and carry her from that moment until she took her final breath.

The strength, peace, and joy that radiated from her as she walked her cancer journey was because her hand was always in the hand of Jesus. He also carried me as I cared for her during this precious season in both of our lives. When the time came for her to leave for heaven, He comforted and sustained me as I had to accept that I would not see my best friend, my beautiful mother, until I walk through the gates of heaven myself one day. He is the One who carried me when it was all too much to bear on my own.

Sometimes in this life we are given more than we can handle. And oftentimes we try to carry our burdens in our own strength. Oh, but we don't have to, friend. In our struggles, suffering, and day-to-day trials, even unto death, He gives us Himself.

If the burdens are heavy, if your cares are weighing painfully on your heart and on your soul, if you are carrying more than you can bear, today, in this moment, hand over every weight and burden to the Lord. Ask Him to help you let go and release each one. Ask Him to help you feel and trust that He is carrying you now and will carry you through.

We don't endure alone. We have the Lord, who daily bears our burdens and who will sustain us, always and forever.

Father,

I realize I am carrying more than I can handle. I cannot do this on my own. I need Your help.

I cling to the truth that You will carry me and that You daily bear my burdens (Psalm 68:19). This morning I release my burdens and cares over to You. If I attempt to pick them back up, may Your Holy Spirit help me release them yet again.

The weight of my burdens has diminished my strength. Would You strengthen me again, Father? As You take my burdens, would You bring a lightness to me today? Would You help me remember that I am Your daughter and that I can rest in Your arms as You carry me?

I love You. In Jesus' name I pray, amen.

A Bruised Reed He Will Not Break

"A bruised reed he will not break, and a smoldering wick he will not quench."

MATTHEW 12:20

Evening

I remember this verse speaking to my heart after my mama passed away. This is how I felt, like a "bruised reed," bruised not only by grief but also by the tremendous amount of stress that comes from putting things in order after someone passes away.

I held on so tightly to this promise that He wouldn't allow me to break. And He was true to His Word, as always. He strengthened and refreshed me. He taught me to go to Him when I am bruised by life's painful blows.

I have had other moments of bruising, feeling beaten down and overwhelmed, as if I am about to break. I would repeat "A bruised reed He will not break" over and over in my mind and spirit, reminding myself that He had held me together before, He didn't allow me to break before, He didn't leave me in my bruising and weakness before, and He wouldn't leave me now.

In this verse, Matthew was quoting a prophecy from Isaiah 42:1–9. This prophecy spoke to the character, purpose, gentleness, and righteousness of the Servant of the Lord, the Messiah to come, whom we now know to be Jesus Christ. It is clear throughout the ministry of Jesus how He loved and cared for those who were "bruised reeds." When you feel bruised by life, almost to your breaking point, Jesus holds you together and infuses His strength and healing into your wounds and weakness. Your bruises He will tend to, your bruises He will heal. It's astounding how loved we are by Him.

The burdens we try to carry bruise us and threaten to break us, but He is the One who carries us and who carries our burdens. We will not break under the weight because we no longer carry the burden. We may be bruised, but we will not be broken, because we know He is faithful to His promises.

Jesus,

You were bruised beyond what I can fathom: for me, for my sins. By Your wounds I have been healed, healed from a life of sin and darkness. I have been made new, washed in Your love and righteousness. Your wounds have healed mine.

For the joy set before You, You surrendered to bruising, to suffering, to death by crucifixion. Why? Because of Your incomprehensible love. Your love for my soul, saving me for eternity and keeping me from breaking in this present time, when I feel bruised and weakened by life's journey.

I trust You, Lord, to be my strength. When I feel as though I am about to break, help me to know You are near and bring to mind Your promises. I am so grateful for You, my Savior. Amen.

For I, the Lᴏʀᴅ your God, hold your right hand; it is I
who say to you, "Fear not, I am the one who helps you."

Isaiah 41:13

When Prayers Are Not Answered in the Way We Had Hoped

In the day when I cried out, You answered me, and
made me bold with strength in my soul.

PSALM 138:3 NKJV

Morning

One of the greatest prayers I have ever prayed, continually
and ardently, weeping often as I petitioned God, was for
the healing of my mother.

One day my aunt unexpectedly messaged me that my mom
was in the hospital and explained the symptoms she was having. I felt the Holy Spirit in that moment prepare me that it
was cancer before any diagnosis was confirmed. Twelve years
earlier, my dad had passed away from cancer, and here I was
now trying to comprehend my mother having it as well. The
pain was excruciating. I could hardly breathe from crying. For
hours, all I could do was get on my knees or lie on the floor,
praying and worshiping.

The next day, I woke up with an entirely different coun-
tenance and perspective. I flew out to Dallas, where my mom
lived, filled with an overwhelming joy and peace unlike anything I had ever experienced. The Lord filled my mind with
thoughts of the beauty of heaven; He filled me with a type of

strength I know comes only from Him. He walked alongside me as I began to walk alongside her through her cancer treatments. And He held my hand while I held hers as she left this earthly phase and breathed her first heavenly breath.

While the Lord did not answer my prayer for her healing and extension of life, He did answer by gifting me with a new, forever changed perspective on life, eternity, and His goodness. He answered with His strength, comfort, and joy even through the valley of the shadow of death. He answered by remaining faithful to the greatest promise He has given all Christians—she was now in heaven with Him.

There are still moments I cry and struggle to understand why it had to be this way. Could it have been a different way? What I rest upon is His sovereignty and His eternal plan. And although we cannot fully understand the ways in which He works, what's beautiful is the invitation to draw near and be comforted by the One who does understand it all.

For His plans are good and trustworthy; He works all things together for the good of those who love Him (Romans 8:28). So when you don't understand, may this promise in His Word bring your heart consolation.

Look also to these reassuring words in Scripture to see how God responds to our desperate prayers:

"I am with you" (Isaiah 41:10 NIV).
"I will strengthen you" (Isaiah 41:10 NIV).
"I will help you" (Isaiah 41:13 NIV).

"I will give you rest" (Matthew 11:28).

"Never will I leave you; never will I forsake you"
(Hebrews 13:5 NIV).

Lord,

When I pray "Your will be done," I truly mean it. I pray Your will be done in my life and on earth as it is in heaven. So when You answer a prayer of mine in a different way than I had hoped, I trust Your sovereignty, perspective, and goodness. Despite the suffering and heartbreak this answer may bring, I trust You to relieve my sorrow.

O Lord, it can be so painful at times. I don't have to push my pain aside. No, I can be honest and vulnerable with You.

I will never fully understand Your ways and what You allow. Yet my pain settles itself within the grand sky, within the vast sea of Your peace and Your love. Amen.

The Gift of Prayer

Because he bends down to listen, I will pray as long
as I have breath!

PSALM 116:2 NLT

Evening

What do we do when our prayers are not answered in the
way we had hoped? Do we get angry at God? Do we
draw near to Him or turn away? Do we accept His invitation
to trust Him more deeply? Do we end up missing the true gift
of prayer?

The gift of prayer isn't always in the answer; oftentimes it's
God's comfort, His peace, and His nearness that become the
gift. *He* is the gift.

To know that we can pray to our holy and powerful God,
and that He bends down to listen, overwhelms my soul. While
I'm so thankful when prayers are answered in the way I had
hoped, I don't want to miss or take for granted the profoundly
beautiful gift of really experiencing Him as I pray and commune with Him. There is no greater love felt than when He is
near in moments of deep need when I'm hurting or worried.

It's okay to be sad and disappointed when our prayers are
not answered in the way we so desperately hoped for. It is okay
to hurt and cry. We can bring our tears and questions and

pain to Him. I implore both myself and you to go to Him, seek Him, seek His face. These are the moments that can deepen our relationship with Him and comfort our souls like nothing else can or ever will.

He is the Great I Am. And the Great I Am has given us the immense gift of prayer. The gift of Him calling us to come and present our requests to Him. The gift of intimacy with Him. The gift of getting to know His character more and more. We seek God in prayer not just to receive something from Him but to give Him something—to give Him praise, adoration, worship, thanksgiving, devotion. When we hear His encouragement to come and talk with Him, may our hearts respond eagerly, "LORD, I am coming" (Psalm 27:8 NLT).

Lord,

    Thank You for Your great gift of prayer. Thank You that You call me to You, that You tell my heart to come and talk with You. Oh, how I don't ever want to take prayer for granted, how I never want to miss out on the true gift of prayer!

    You know the pain I've felt when prayers were not answered in the way I so desperately hoped for, yet I have seen, in the middle of a broken heart and in the middle of my tears, that underneath is a peace that testifies to Your presence.

I see that the true gift of prayer is You. My kind, ever-present, cherished God. The treasure of being near You is the greatest treasure of all. Amen.

"I have said these things to you, that in me you may have peace. In the world you will have tribulation. But take heart; I have overcome the world."

John 16:33

The Lifter of Your Head

But you, O LORD, are a shield about me, my glory,
and the lifter of my head.

PSALM 3:3

Morning

This morning you may have woken up with your mind and heart weighed down. When your head is heavy from troubles and afflictions, the Lord is the One who lifts your head. And when your head lifts, who do you see? You see Him. You see His eyes looking into yours. You see His face, radiant with glory, mercy, and love. This is the God we serve and adore. He is not a distant God; He is a compassionate God.

When your heart is weighed down by worries and despair, He is the only One who can relieve your sorrows with the greatest of care. Throughout Scripture, God reveals to us just how near He is, how intimately and personally involved He is in our lives and the lives of His people.

Consider the story of Job. Though his suffering was great, God made Himself known in a greater way to Job in his suffering. As Job said, "I had heard of you by the hearing of the ear, but now my eye sees you" (Job 42:5). It is the same for us: in our suffering, He reveals Himself to us in a more intimate way.

God often becomes more real to us in our suffering. I've known His strength when I felt like I couldn't get up from the bathroom floor after weeping, and I've felt His peace and joy that didn't make sense in the middle of my pain. Can you think of a time when you saw God lifting you up, when the only way you made it through was with Him by your side? He always has been and always will be the Lifter of our head.

The Lord is the One who alleviates our pain and remains with us in our suffering. God didn't abandon Job in his afflictions, and He doesn't abandon us in ours. May we, like Job, be steadfast during our trials. "Behold, we consider those blessed who remained steadfast. You have heard of the steadfastness of Job, and you have seen the purpose of the Lord, how the Lord is compassionate and merciful" (James 5:11).

How blessed we are to have the tender affections of God. When we fall, He upholds us; when we are bowed down, He raises us up (Psalm 145:14). He lifts our head, and in our suffering, we see Him. Today we can join with all of heaven and earth to delight in this truth: "Shout for joy, you heavens; rejoice, you earth; burst into song, you mountains! For the LORD comforts his people and will have compassion on his afflicted ones" (Isaiah 49:13 NIV).

The One who lifts my head,

I breathe in, pause, and breathe out, surrendering the things that are weighing on my mind and my heart this morning. Help me slow down today and notice the sweetness of life and the blessings You bestow, even during trying times.

Thank You, God, for bringing me closer to Your heart in my suffering, Your affection made known in my afflictions. You are the Lifter of my head, the One I see when I look up, the One whose compassions are new every morning. Amen.

The Strength of Your Heart

My flesh and my heart may fail, but God is the
strength of my heart and my portion forever.

PSALM 73:26

Evening

Many times in life we come to the end of ourselves, to the end of our strength. In our humanness, we need to be refreshed by God's strength daily. Sometimes we forget to ask God for His help, or we begin to strive, attempting to do things in our own strength, whether we realize it or not. When we try to power through, we inevitably become weak, depleted, or anxious because we are not resting in the promise of God to be our never-ending, always-available strength. His strength never runs out, while ours always does.

Think of a strong, sturdy tree. What keeps the tree stable, secure, and anchored is its roots. The roots hold it up day in and day out, through weather, storms, and years. The strength of the tree lies in the roots, similar to how our strength lies in God.

Scripture paints a beautiful image of God intentionally searching for those who need His strength: "The eyes of the LORD search the whole earth in order to strengthen those whose hearts are fully committed to him" (2 Chronicles 16:9

NLT). The Lord never tires of us going to Him to be the strength of our hearts.

The Lord gives us strength to endure things we never thought we could. This strength looks different on different occasions. Sometimes it is courage to stand strong in a situation, sometimes it is strength to cling to Him through tears, sometimes it is strength to let go and let Him carry us. In His providence and grace, He knows the type of strength we need.

When you need strength, where do you go? Who or what do you depend on in times of weakness? Do you go to God first to share about your trials, or do you first share with others? Do you often look to yourself or to the Lord to strengthen your heart?

We are encouraged by His Word to seek Him and His strength, to seek His presence continually (1 Chronicles 16:11). May this inspire us to draw closer to God and stay close. Strength is found in our seeking of Him and in our longing for His presence. So we kneel before our Creator, who has the strength to uphold the entire universe, declaring that He is the One we entirely rely upon.

And what He provides for the reliant ones is truly wonderful: "He gives strength to the weary and increases the power of the weak. Even youths grow tired and weary, and young men stumble and fall; but those who hope in the LORD will renew their strength. They will soar on wings like eagles; they will run and not grow weary, they will walk and not be faint" (Isaiah 40:29–31 NIV).

Tonight, before falling asleep, recall a time when God gave you strength you knew without a doubt was His and not your own. May this be an encouragement to continue leaning on Him, the strength of your heart.

Lord,

I come to You tonight weary and weak. Please strengthen me while I sleep. Please renew my strength day by day, moment by moment, for I am completely dependent upon You. It's never by my strength, only by Your love, that I endure.

A hymn of praise surfaces in my soul as I reflect on Your faithfulness to hold me up through life's journey. You are the strength of my heart. You are my hope, my refuge, my rock. You are my joy, my treasure, my portion forever. "I love you, O LORD, my strength" (Psalm 18:1). Amen.

I love you, O LORD, my strength.

Psalm 18:1

The Music of Morning

But I will sing of your strength; I will sing aloud
of your steadfast love in the morning. For you
have been to me a fortress and a refuge in the day
of my distress.

PSALM 59:16

Morning

Many mornings I find myself talking with God as I'm in and out of waking up, processing things with Him through prayer. And sometimes I find my thoughts beginning to run ahead of me, thinking of the things I need to do, distracting me from these precious beginning-of-the-day moments with the Lord. Maybe you're the same?

Our hearts are sensitive in the morning hour, and it feels like we are especially susceptible to what we encounter upon waking. Do we abruptly start the day with worries, concerns, to-do lists, emails, social media, the news? It's important to protect our souls in these moments by beginning the day as we were created to—in worship. This welcomes the day with more peace and prepares us to walk in worship throughout the day.

Worship is not only singing or listening to worship music. It is also a heart posture of adoration and praise, acknowledging God's greatness and sovereignty and praising Him as the Lord of our lives. We can worship with our thoughts, our words, our prayers, our singing, our listening, our writing, our reading. We can worship with our work and our rest and every moment in between.

A morning can greet us with either refreshment or weariness, joy or dread, peace or worry. When we feel dread or worry as we start the day, worship can greatly alter the state of our hearts. When we worship in the middle of worry, something supernatural happens because worship weakens worry. It takes our eyes off our temporary struggles to focus on Him and His eternal goodness, glory, and grace.

Remember the promise of 2 Corinthians 4:17–18: "For our light and momentary troubles are achieving for us an eternal glory that far outweighs them all. So we fix our eyes not on what is seen, but on what is unseen, since what is seen is temporary, but what is unseen is eternal" (NIV). Our day's troubles will not last forever, but our worship will echo into eternity.

Lord,

In the morning hours, before I get out of bed, may my heart begin to worship You. And may I worship You throughout the day and into the night. For You are worthy!

I am so thankful You created me to worship. It brings the deepest peace, joy, and purpose to my life. I pray the Holy Spirit would increase even more my desire and capacity to worship upon waking. I want to be a woman whose life is marked by worship. For a worship-filled heart is pleasing to You, God.

Each day, may I wake with worship, making music for You with my words, my praises, my prayers. May my lips, my heart, and my thoughts glorify You. I love You, and I pray my love for You would be apparent in my worship of You. In Jesus' name I pray, amen.

The Symphony of Faith

I keep my eyes always on the LORD. With him at my right hand, I will not be shaken.

PSALM 16:8 NIV

——— *Evening* ———

A conductor stands facing the orchestra, directing each musician with the movement of the baton in his hand. Aside from the sheet music set before them, the musicians' eyes look to the conductor. The conductor brings unity to the music, leading the orchestra members to play in harmony with one another.

Imagine if the musicians began to take their eyes off the conductor and look to the audience for their cues, allowing the reactions or applause of the audience to affect their performance of the symphony. Disunity and confusion would ensue.

As followers of Christ, Jesus is our Conductor, the One who leads us, directs us, unites us. We must keep our eyes on Him. We follow Jesus, not the world, the audience in this metaphor. We are playing the symphony of Christ's love to a watching world. If we begin to watch the reactions of the audience, we will become distracted, easily led astray, anxious, and confused. This affects the whole body of Christ, just as one musician's distraction can affect the depth, beauty, and power of the orchestra's performance.

We are chosen by Jesus, who is both the Conductor and the Composer, and the Word of God is our sheet music. We are each given different instruments with the purpose and ability to play in one accord the symphony of our faith. Think of the most beautiful music that deeply moves your soul. Greater than that should be the music that is our faith. It is a musical composition that is worship to His ears, one that is played for all to hear and can change hearts like no other.

Consider the beauty that comes when we are unified, the heavenly song that would reach the ears of those who have yet to know Him. Consider the testimony of our peace when we keep our eyes on Jesus. Consider our witness to those in the audience of the world struggling with worry and anxiety, encouraging them to also trust in the Conductor and Composer of our faith.

Jesus,

You are the great Conductor and Composer, the One my eyes continually look to. You direct, I follow. Thank You that You have called me to be one of Your instruments and that You have gifted me a family of others in Your orchestra. Collectively we play the melody of grace.

I think of the prayer You prayed to the Father for our unity (John 17:20–23). Our unity is imperative to our testimony of who You are. Forgive us for our disunity. I pray by the power of Your Spirit that we as believers would remain in one accord.

Help us to not become distracted by the watching world but to keep our eyes attentive to Your leading as You guide us in harmony with one another. Every note matters in Your composition, every line tells the story of Your kindness, every instrument has been intentionally selected by You. The entirety of Your symphony tells of Your love not only to the orchestra but also to the watching audience.

Thank You for the music that is our faith, Your masterpiece of mercy. Amen.

O Lord, you are my God; I will exalt you; I will
praise your name, for you have done wonderful
things, plans formed of old, faithful and sure.

Isaiah 25:1

The Steadfast Love of the Lord

It is good to give thanks to the LORD, to sing
praises to your name, O Most High; to declare your
steadfast love in the morning, and your faithfulness
by night.

PSALM 92:1–2

Morning

In the morning, it is good to awaken our hearts with the truth of God's steadfast, unceasing love. It is fitting for our souls to give thanks to the One who embraces us with a love that never ends. Because in a world marked by brokenness, we need to remind ourselves of His love as an unfailing source of comfort and joy.

God's love pours out of His very nature, for "God is love" (1 John 4:16). His love is a devoted love, an intimate love. It is a love that surpasses knowledge (Ephesians 3:17–19). It is a love that is inseparable: "Neither death nor life, nor angels nor rulers, nor things present nor things to come, nor powers, nor height nor depth, nor anything else in all creation, will be able to separate us from the love of God in Christ Jesus our Lord" (Romans 8:38–39).

No greater act shows God's faithful love for us than His sending of Jesus: "In this the love of God was made manifest among us, that God sent his only Son into the world, so that we might live through him" (1 John 4:9). Jesus came in human form, demonstrating so deeply, so profoundly, so sacrificially the love God has for us. A love so unlike anything of this world, so precious and pure, holy and good. A love that David boldly proclaimed is "better than life" (Psalm 63:3).

When we declare His love each morning, our thoughts fill with His goodness and kindness, giving us hope and strength as the day begins. His love continues to pull us close to Him and sets our hearts on living each day with Him and for Him. All His decisions and plans for your life are rooted in His great love. You are protected by His love, led by His love, strengthened by His love, refreshed by His love, saved by His love, kept by His love, calmed by His love.

May you start every day afresh in God's lovingkindness. I pray the Lord would direct your heart to the love of God and to the steadfastness of Christ this morning and every morning (2 Thessalonians 3:5).

Lord,

   What better way to begin my day than by meditating on Your love. Your heart contains a love that cannot sufficiently be explained by the human language. A love that is enduring and everlasting.

   Your love holds me, it carries me, it sustains me. Your love is what keeps me breathing. Thank You for loving me, thank You that nothing can separate me from Your steadfast love. Thank You for my heart's ability to love You in return.

   May Your love never cease to amaze me. And may my lips ever praise You because Your steadfast love is better than life (Psalm 63:3)! Amen.

Recounting His Faithfulness Like Counting Stars

Your steadfast love, O LORD, extends to the heavens, your faithfulness to the clouds.

PSALM 36:5

Evening

I remember lying on the boat deck of my husband's family's lake house one summer night in northern Michigan. Thousands of stars filled the night sky, more than I had ever seen. I couldn't begin to count them! I was in awe as the stars collectively and joyfully displayed His majesty. As they lit up the sky, each star reflected God's glory.

Just as it is good to declare His steadfast love in the morning, it is good also to declare His faithfulness at night (Psalm 92:2), ending the day considering the ways God has been faithful. When we say God is faithful, it means God is always true to His Word and His character. Testimonies of God's faithfulness have been written throughout the Bible and are still being written throughout our stories today. Trying to count the stories that remind us of why God can be trusted is like counting the stars in the sky: we never run out of testimonies that help us remember.

One story that testifies to His faithfulness is His healing

and transformation in my own marriage. I was in my mid-twenties when my dad was diagnosed with cancer and passed away three months later. This was twelve years before losing my mom to cancer. After my dad passed away, I was not tending to my grief. Instead, I made it worse by going out and drinking a lot, trying to numb the pain. My now-husband, Michael, and I met a year later through a mutual friend at a bar and built our relationship on going out. While we did have fun together and loved being with one another, it wasn't the foundation needed to begin a healthy marriage. The first three years of our marriage were incredibly hard, to the point that I often thought we would get divorced.

Mercifully, God, in His kindness, presented an opportunity for us to move from our home in Chicago to Dallas. It meant leaving behind our going-out lifestyle, which caused a massive drop-off in our drinking. In the calm and quiet, God began to heal the layers of my grief, drawing me back to Himself and deeply growing my faith. Simultaneously, He was tending to Michael's heart, faithfully redeeming what was broken within us and in our marriage. We sought God, rebuilding the foundation of our marriage on Him, and He gifted us with a greater love for one another. He made us new and our marriage new. Now, by His grace, we have been together for well over a decade (nearly fourteen years as I write this!).

Just as the stars are impossible to count, so, too, are the examples of God's faithfulness. There is never a shortage of all the ways in which He is faithful. His faithfulness is immeasurable, His promises abundant. Our God has been faithful throughout the generations and will be always and forever. It is who He is.

As you fall asleep tonight, begin to recount God's faithfulness in your life. May remembering that He keeps His promises strengthen your heart to know His faithfulness will greet you again tomorrow and the next day and for all the days of your life. Just as we are in awe of the many stars He has created, may we be in awe of His abundant faithfulness.

Lord,

I recount Your faithfulness as I lay my head on my pillow tonight. As I recall Your faithfulness in the past, my soul rests, trusting in Your future faithfulness.

I pray the troubles of my heart would be washed away as I meditate on Your promises, remembering how You've always been with me and will be with me again tomorrow. My heart is calmed as I consider how You, who spoke the stars into existence, are abundant in faithfulness.

You are faithful every day, every hour, every minute. It's who You are. All praise and honor belong to You, my faithful God. I love You so much, amen.

When Everything Feels Out of Control

My thoughts are not your thoughts, neither are your ways my ways, declares the LORD. For as the heavens are higher than the earth, so are my ways higher than your ways and my thoughts than your thoughts.

ISAIAH 55:8–9

Morning

Life so often feels out of our control. In truth, most of life *is* out of our control. There are some painful seasons or experiences when we especially struggle with not being able to control or change our circumstances, which leaves us confused, anxious, and disheartened. From our viewpoint, it's hard to make sense of it.

I have been through a several-years-long course of learning I am not in control, from losing both of my parents to cancer, to struggling with infertility, to the ups and downs of our adoption journey. I did what I could within each of these circumstances—I prayed, researched, sought the expertise of doctors, looked into treatment plans—but ultimately, the outcome was up to God. It was hard not to desire more control. I so desperately wished there was something more I could do to make those situations feel less chaotic and heartbreaking. But I realized the best thing for me to do was surrender because, in every circumstance, each heartache was building my faith and deepening my trust in God. The more I surrendered, the more peace I felt.

God is the One in control, better at governing it all than we could ever be. His ways are perfect and good. This doesn't always mean they *feel* good, but we can still trust they are because God is good. He never abandons us while we wrestle to try and understand. He carries us through by His love, and He changes our perspective by His grace. He transforms us, making us more into the likeness of Christ, when we can say in humility, "Nevertheless, not my will, but yours, be done" (Luke 22:42).

God allowed Job to endure great suffering and loss (Job 1–2); He allowed Hannah to be barren for many years (1 Samuel 1); He allowed Daniel to be thrown into the lions' den (Daniel 6); He allowed Joseph to be sold into slavery (Genesis 37:18–36) and unjustly placed in prison (39:19–21); He allowed Paul to be a prisoner and be shipwrecked on his way to Rome (Acts 27). While these circumstances and events were out of their control, God's great purposes were unfolding. The Lord restored and healed, comforted and blessed, rescued and gave honor. His justice and mercy prevailed, and His power and grace brought salvation.

We can find courage from those who have gone before us when certain moments in life feel so painfully out of our control. We can keep trusting in the sovereign plans and deep love of the Lord.

Lord,

When everything feels out of control and it doesn't make sense, please calm my heart. When circumstances are painful, please give me grace to trust You more.

Surrendering is not always easy, and when it's not, please help me abandon my false sense of control, taking hold of Your hand and Your peace instead.

I find rest and hope this morning that You are in control and I am not. Amen.

Ten Thousand Things

And we know that for those who love God all things
work together for good, for those who are called
according to his purpose.

ROMANS 8:28

Evening

God is doing so much behind the scenes that we may never know about or see in this life. John Piper captured this so well when he said, "God is always doing 10,000 things in your life, and you may be aware of three of them."[6] We cannot even scratch the surface of grasping all that is in His control, both in our lives and the entire universe.

I love jigsaw puzzles. And I couldn't help but think of Piper's words in terms of puzzle pieces. I envisioned God putting together a 10,000-piece puzzle, doing it at His perfect pace within His perfect sovereignty. It was a puzzle He alone could fully see, and although I could see only three pieces, I still trusted that the whole puzzle was coming together. And I knew it was for my benefit that He didn't reveal it to me all at once.

In life, God knows the big picture and exactly how all the pieces will perfectly fit together. We are shown only a few pieces, giving us glimpses of the puzzle He is intently and affectionately completing. So pause and ask yourself: Can I be satisfied that only God knows what the final masterpiece is? Can I be content with just seeing a few pieces of the puzzle? Can I make peace with not knowing all He is doing behind the scenes, trusting He is in control of the bigger picture?

As His children, we take one day at a time with our Father, abiding in His sovereignty. We cannot see the whole picture, so we seek the guidance and wisdom of the One who does. Proverbs says, "Many are the plans in a person's heart, but it is the LORD's purpose that prevails" (19:21 NIV). While it isn't bad to make plans, we should do so through prayer while holding our plans loosely. We do not know what tomorrow will bring—only He does—so we continue to say, "If the Lord wills, we will live and do this or that" (James 4:15). Don't hold too tightly to attempts to control life and daily plans, because it can rob you from living in the peace that comes with trusting God.

Instead, know that day by day, piece by piece, God's good plans will be accomplished in your life. He is in control, working behind the scenes. He is leading you as He intentionally fits each puzzle piece of your life together, designing it all out of His faithfulness and love.

Lord,

In Your hand is the life of every living thing and the breath of all mankind (Job 12:10).

Your ways of governing life are perfect. My very breath is in Your hands—how can I not trust You with everything, Lord?

Day by day, I seek Your will and wisdom, guidance and grace. Lead me as I make plans, and help me hold them loosely.

Although I do not see the whole picture, I am at peace knowing that You work all things together for good. I rely on You as You work behind the scenes, not only fitting together the puzzle of my life but also fitting all of our lives together into a much grander picture to display Your glory. Amen.

In the multitude of my anxieties within
me, Your comforts delight my soul.

Psalm 94:19 NKJV

When the Cares of Your Heart Are Many

When the cares of my heart are many,
your consolations cheer my soul.

PSALM 94:19

Morning

So much is happening in the world on a global, national, and personal scale. Sometimes it feels like we can't go a day without something attempting to fill us with worry, fear, heaviness, or sorrow. But as care upon care begins to weigh on our hearts, Scripture reminds us time and time again to pray and seek the One who can truly comfort and uplift our souls. Another translation of Psalm 94:19 shares this sentiment in such a lovely way: "In the multitude of my anxieties within me, Your comforts delight my soul" (NKJV). From the heavy weight of many cares to the deep joy of His consolations, His presence ushers in peace.

Have you ever experienced the joy and peace that come from sitting in the Lord's presence and turning all your cares over to Him? One day as I was praying, I felt God invite me to share with Him all the worries in my heart. I thought I had surrendered them to Him already. But the Holy Spirit revealed I was still holding on to them and encouraged me to pray through and hand over each worry. Once I gave those fears, worries, and burdens to Him, I experienced the promised peace of God relieving my heart.

Philippians 4:6–7 instructs us what to do when the cares of our hearts are many: "Do not be anxious about anything, but in everything by prayer and supplication with thanksgiving let your requests be made known to God. And the peace of God, which surpasses all understanding, will guard your hearts and your minds in Christ Jesus."

In this passage, we see that the relief, comfort, and answers all lie within Him. We pray, laying our requests before Him, humbly asking Him to help us. The Greek word translated here as *supplication* refers to a "heart-felt petition, arising out of deep personal need."[7] What a perfect word to express our state of being when our cares are many. Philippians 4:6–7 also says to let our requests be made known with thanksgiving. Why might that be? In the middle of feeling anxious, my natural inclination is to focus more on what I'm worried about than on giving thanks to God.

Yet when we approach God with thankfulness, a heart shift begins. It enables us to pause our anxious thoughts and, instead, fill our minds with thoughts of God and His goodness. Thanking God in the middle of feeling worried makes room for peace in your soul. I've been working on thanking God in the middle of feeling worried. I push aside the anxiety by sharing with Him the things I'm grateful for, and it significantly changes my perspective and reminds me of His faithfulness. Thankfulness proves to be a balm for the anxious heart.

This morning, as you pray, identify what you are anxious about. Hand over every worry. Release your grip, and empty your heart of all the cares you're carrying. With thanksgiving let your requests be made known to God. As this becomes a continual practice, the treasure of consolations in God multiplies.

My Lord, my Consoler,

When the cares of my heart are many, You are the One who comforts my soul.

You are my lasting comfort. Nothing else cheers my soul like You do. Nothing else encourages my heart to keep going like You do. Nothing else diminishes my anxieties like You do.

May Your Spirit remind me to pray and release any worry or care to You. Help me to not be anxious about anything but lay my requests before You with an offering of thanksgiving. Because yes, Lord, I am so thankful for You and the abundance of Your love, grace, and blessings.

Your consolations delight my soul and take away the troubles of my heart. Amen.

The God Who Cares for You

Cast all your anxiety on him because he cares for you.

1 PETER 5:7 NIV

Evening

W hat a precious promise! God cares for us. This verse could have stated a variety of reasons why we should cast all our anxieties on Him, but highlighted here is one central reason: He cares for us. This is what God wanted to speak through Peter, a reassurance that He is there, a loving statement by our Father.

Consider a child who is worried or fearful about something, and a parent out of love and care says, "Share your worries with me. I will help you through them." Even at my daughter Norah's young age, when she gets startled and scared by a loud noise and begins to cry, I immediately console her. And as she grows up, I will continue to comfort her and speak truth into her worries because of how much I love her.

It's out of God's love for us that He tells us to give Him our anxiety. This comforting truth has the power to reframe our perspective. Since He cares so deeply for us, why do we continue to allow cares to make their way so often and easily into our hearts? When I forget about God's care, I miss out on a tremendous amount of peace. I tend to lay down a worry and then pick it back up again, falling back into trying to manage on my own. Maybe you struggle with this too. We strive or push ourselves to figure it out, exhausting ourselves, instead of exhaling and trusting that the One who cares for us will work it all out.

God never tires of our need for Him. He is always there, always willing. And it brings Him joy when we seek Him and call out to Him for help. Our relationship with Him builds upon this humble act of reliance and dependence. Sometimes we fall into the rhythm of coping in our own ways, but these ways will leave us burdened and empty, whereas God lightens and refills.

It is good to persistently acknowledge any worries or fears and keep casting each one on God by faith. The word *cast* holds within it intentionality and force. Think of a shot put from a track and field event, where the athlete "casts" or throws a heavy ball as far as possible. If we are casting all our anxieties on Him, they should be out of arm's reach so we cannot pick them up again. And when casting our worries is not easy for us, let's ask God to give us the strength to throw them off, entirely and completely.

His very nature speaks to His care for us. He is a faithful God, gracious and kind, abounding in steadfast love. He knows we are weak, and He knows in this life we will have troubles. We are sustained by His care; we survive by His care. If He promises to take care of us, why do we wrestle within ourselves instead of letting Him care for us? Friend, we can stop wrestling with our worries and rest in His care.

Father,

Sometimes I attempt to handle my cares on my own, not trusting You as I should. Please forgive me. Sometimes I hand You a worry and then take it back again. Please forgive me.

Please give me the strength to cast all my cares on You. Help me to not depend on my own way of managing worries but to go to You, the One on whom I lean.

Because You care for me, You tell me not to be anxious. Because You love me, You take my cares upon Yourself. In Scripture I see Your care for others throughout every page. In my life I see Your care throughout every day. I love You. Amen.

Tending to Your Tears

You have kept count of my tossings; put my tears in
your bottle. Are they not in your book?

PSALM 56:8

Morning

One night a couple of years ago, I cried one of the hard-
est cries of my life. The grief of losing my parents, my
longing for children still at the age of forty-one, the pressure
I was feeling to perform professionally, and a physical pain I
was healing from all came together. It was too much. I had
been holding in my tears, trying to cope by pushing through
instead of being honest and raw with the Lord about how much
pain I was in.

But this particular night I no longer held in my tears. They
needed to be released—and the Lord was there to catch each
one. It was as though each tear was taking part in the healing
that needed to take place in my heart.

I learned the blessing of vulnerability before the Lord that
night. I learned that it is honoring to Him when we bring Him
our tears in prayer, with many words or with few. I needed to
cry—and I needed my Father.

Sometimes we need to be reminded that it's okay to cry,
that it's *good* to cry. In our culture there is often pressure to

rush through our weeping and our sorrow. Even in the church, we sometimes fail to make enough room to express suffering.

God gave us the ability to weep and feel and share our pain with Him. When brought to Him, tears are an expression of our intimate trust in God. There is a sacredness to the tears we shed in His presence. Every tear communicates to Him that we are hurting, and His response to every tear is compassion.

Our tears matter to God; His Word tells us so. He collects them, He records them. He isn't too busy, and He doesn't look away. He comes near, so close as to collect each one in His bottle. Our tears stir His sympathy toward us.

David wept. Job wept. Joseph wept. Jeremiah wept. Hannah wept. Mary, the sister of Lazarus, wept. Paul served with tears. We see throughout Scripture that there are times in a faithful walk when tears fall, and they have a safe place to land.

Let us also remember the shortest verse in the Bible: "Jesus wept" (John 11:35). Two words, but oh the significance in just two words. This verse captures the response of Jesus to the death of Lazarus, His follower and friend. Even though He knew He was about to resurrect Lazarus and turn mourning into joy, He didn't skip over this moment to share in the sorrow of those who despaired. Our Consoler knows sorrow and suffering. His time on earth shows that if He can weep, so can we.

If you're holding in tears, go to your Heavenly Father. Nothing else in this world compares to His comfort. You are His child. He loves you. You are not alone in your tears. Your tears are tended to by God.

My compassionate God,

Help me to let go of the tears I've been holding in as I come to You, my Father, the One who comforts me in all my afflictions.

You gave us the ability to cry, an expression of our sorrow and sadness and a response to life's suffering. Tears sown with You reap something beautiful, something I don't think we will fully understand until eternity.

You collect my tears in Your bottle; You have recorded them in Your book. I am never alone in my suffering.

May my tears water my faith and grow me more into Christ's likeness. May my tears nourish my relationship with You, drawing us closer to one another. Amen.

Releasing and Receiving

In my distress I called upon the LORD; to my God I
cried for help. From his temple he heard my voice,
and my cry to him reached his ears.

PSALM 18:6

Evening

When we don't have words and can come to God only
with tears as our prayers, God still hears and brings
relief. Like a rainbow after a storm or a flower blooming after
the rain, there is renewed hope after our stored-up tears are
given their needed opportunity to fall. When we give Him
our tears and pain, we make room for God to lighten our
despair and bring peace to our hearts. Laying our pain at His
feet gives us open hands to receive His peace, strength, and
comfort.

This simple idea of releasing in order to receive is present
throughout life, even in our own lungs. With every breath, we
release carbon dioxide to take in oxygen. If we are holding in
our breath, we cannot receive the oxygen we need. God created this perfect cycle of breathing, of releasing and receiving,
which physically sustains us. We can apply this idea to our
spiritual health: exhaling our pain, tears, worries, or fears
and inhaling God's love, healing, and peace. And as we move

throughout our days, inhaling and exhaling, we continue this cycle of releasing and receiving.

Sometimes when we pray for God's help, strength, peace, and so on, we may falsely believe we also have to work for those things. The truth is, they are gifts to receive from a good Father who renews, refreshes, and restores us as we go to Him.

After the emotional, tearful time I spent with the Lord that I mentioned this morning, He then brought me the words of the prayer I've written below. In the releasing and receiving, God guided me to what He wanted to give me. The words of this prayer felt like breathing in fresh, cool, reviving air. I pray it will be the same for you tonight.

Lord,
> *I receive Your love.*
> *I receive Your peace.*
> *I receive Your hope.*
> *I receive Your healing.*
> *I receive Your refreshment.*
> *I receive Your guidance.*
> *I receive Your grace.*
> *I receive Your wisdom.*

I receive Your strength.

I receive Your comfort.

I receive Your blessings.

I receive Your _____.

(Add anything else He may be speaking to you personally.)

Amen.

The LORD is near to the brokenhearted
and saves the crushed in spirit.

Psalm 34:18 ESV

He Heals the Brokenhearted

He heals the brokenhearted and binds up their
wounds.

PSALM 147:3 NIV

Morning

Several years ago my husband and I rang in the New Year
in a vastly different way than any previous New Year. It
was the most painful but the most meaningful. Right before
New Year's Eve, I did something to my neck that caused a
severe strain. I don't think anything in my life had ever been
so physically painful. I had to go to the ER, where I was given
a muscle relaxant and pain relievers, which helped, but I could
still feel the pain. The most concerning part was my history of
a carotid artery dissection since the pain was in the same area
where the dissection had occurred.

Michael watched over me so intently. He made me food,
washed my hair, helped me walk, carried me when it was especially painful, wiped my tears, and prayed for me day and
night. One night he held my hand the entire night while we
slept, one of my favorite memories in our marriage to date. As
he cared for me, his love was an outpouring of the Father's love
and a reflection of how the Father tends to our wounds and
brokenness.

To bind up wounds, one must come extremely close to the one who is hurt. One must touch the person as they care for them, serving their needs with the desire to bring comfort and relief. Consider that the Most High God is the One who comes close to tend to our pain and afflictions with the desire to bring comfort and relief. The intimacy of this interaction with God is wonderfully astounding and reassuring.

The Lord draws in the brokenhearted, mending the heart's wounds, wrapping His love around the one who is hurting to heal each broken piece. He formed our hearts, our inner being, and He knows how fragile they can be as we travel through this world. Charles Spurgeon speaks of the ways our hearts may break and the medicine for every type of heartbreak: "Hearts are broken through disappointment. Hearts are broken through bereavement. Hearts are broken in ten thousand ways, for this is a heart-breaking world; and Christ is good at healing all manner of heartbreaks."[8]

Jesus is tender and compassionate and immediately aware the second our hearts break. He moves swiftly in His great sympathy to be our Healer. Our healing is often a process. There are stages of healing, and He comforts and heals through each stage: the initial breaking and the immense pain of the break, the binding, and the lingering soreness that comes with healing. He is, in every aspect, caring for you day by day as He heals and strengthens you.

He is the Creator, Physician, Nurse, and loving Parent all in one. We can trust Him with our broken hearts and wounds.

We can be vulnerable to show Him our wounds and the pieces of our hearts, allowing ourselves to be healed.

If your heart feels broken today or you have wounds that need God's care, God is with you in your hurting. Keep going to Him in the healing process, rest in His care, and trust Him to heal your broken heart and bind up your wounds. Bring all your pain to Him. He loves you; He is near.

Lord,

I hold out the pieces of my broken heart to You. I show You my wounds. Tears come to my eyes as I am in awe that You care so deeply for my broken heart. In Your concern and care, You come close to bandage and look after me as I heal. In my brokenness and woundedness, I am drawn into Your arms.

You dwell with the hurting and afflicted; You are close to the brokenhearted (Psalm 34:18). My wounded heart finds relief in the great sea of Your compassion. And I am healed by the gentle consolation of Your love. Amen.

He Determines the
Number of Stars

He determines the number of the stars and calls
them each by name. Great is our Lord and mighty
in power; his understanding has no limit.

PSALM 147:4–5 NIV

Evening

Have you ever noticed how today's morning and evening verses are placed next to one another in Scripture? Tonight's verses come right after our verse from this morning:

He heals the brokenhearted and binds up their wounds. He determines the number of the stars and calls them each by name. Great is our Lord and mighty in power; his understanding has no limit. (Psalm 147:3–5 NIV)

The message of each verse is so powerful when they're read together. We see in the same breath that the God who determines the number of stars, the One who calls them each by name, the One who is abundant in power, considers our broken hearts valuable and worthy to be healed. How magnificent is our God! How kind is our God! His love is just as great as His power. What could bring more comfort than to be thought of and cared for by this majestic, tender God who is mindful of our broken hearts and who names each star that shines!

There are more than 100 billion stars just in our home galaxy, and "astronomers estimate that the universe could contain up to one septillion stars, that's a one followed by 24 zeros."[9] But the exact number of stars no human knows. The number is always an estimation. Scientists and astronomers go to great lengths to attempt to number the stars. In my search for the answer to how many stars there are, I found myself marveling at God and His Word. As hard as people try, "the stars of the sky cannot be counted" (Jeremiah 33:22 NLT).

Only God can count every star. He doesn't just know the exact number of stars, He determines the number! And He calls them each by name. It could be easy to believe that you and I go unnoticed or ignored when God is governing the entire universe. But that's not the case. He knows every star in the sky by name, and He knows each of us by name. This is the character of God: His glory and love, His delight in and consideration for His creation, His splendor and affection.

May you fall asleep tonight considering the care of the Lord and the grandness of the Lord, that the One who numbers the stars is mindful of you and cares for you. I pray this brings the sweetest peace and sleep tonight.

My God, who numbers the stars,

Your brilliance and glory are reflected in every star. Your majesty surpasses the stars; it's endless. Your love outshines the stars; it's infinite.

"When I consider your heavens, the work of your fingers, the moon and the stars, which you have set in place, what is mankind that you are mindful of them, human beings that you care for them?" (Psalm 8:3–4 NIV). And yet You are mindful of us, You do care for us. You are powerful beyond measure and caring beyond measure.

You know each star, and You know me. Oh, that I would daily desire to know You more deeply! That I would cherish the beauty of abiding in You and with You all the days of my life. Amen.

When I Awake, You Are Still with Me

How precious are your thoughts about me, O God.
They cannot be numbered! I can't even count them;
they outnumber the grains of sand! And when I
wake up, you are still with me!

PSALM 139:17–18 NLT

— *Morning* —

As you woke up this morning, did you consider that God was right there, already with you? That He was thinking of you and your needs for the day ahead? We know that God is omnipresent and omniscient. But do we make personal this truth? He is everywhere, and He is everywhere *with you*. He knows everything, and He knows everything *about you*.

He has known you from the beginning, as He knit you together in your mother's womb, as He fearfully and wonderfully made you (Psalm 139:13–14). As a parent has a multitude of thoughts in loving, caring, and providing for their child, so does God for us, but His thoughts are substantially more—they outnumber the grains of sand. His thoughts of you cannot be numbered. How incredible to think about!

Powerful and personal, infinite and intimate. This is our

God! When we recognize and cherish the presence of God in our lives, we desire to commune with Him.

When we commune with God, we are communicating and conversing with Him throughout the day, sharing our thoughts, needs, thankfulness, and observations. Communing is praying without ceasing—a continual conversation with our closest Companion, Father, and Friend. It's reading His Word and listening for His voice; it's singing and worshiping; it's continually seeking His guidance and will. It's confessing sin as convictions come to our hearts. Communing with God is our greatest joy. It's inviting Him into every aspect of life; it's crying to Him and with Him; it's rejoicing with Him and laughing with Him; it's building and investing in a close relationship— the most important, most precious relationship of our lives.

We were created to commune with God, to have fellowship with Him every moment of every day. Nothing can give peace to our minds and delight to our souls like this gift of fellowship. For if His thoughts of us outnumber the grains of sand, why would we not aim to direct more of our thoughts toward Him?

Each morning, may we begin communing with God upon waking. May our first thoughts be of Him. May we remember He never left us in the night. He is still with us in the morning, and He will be with us throughout the day.

God,

I awake, and You are still with me.

Keep me aware of Your treasured company all through-out the day. You are my greatest Companion, the One who greets me first thing as I open my eyes and who remains with me every moment. May we talk together and walk together throughout the course of the day. How sweet a day is when lived this way.

If I am thought of by You, Lord, how can I not face the day with greater peace?

If I am always with You, Lord, how can I not face the day with greater joy?

Oh, help me to always remember the gift of Your pres-ence. Amen.

One Thing I Have Desired

One thing I have desired of the LORD, that will
I seek: that I may dwell in the house of the LORD
all the days of my life, to behold the beauty of the
LORD, and to inquire in His temple.

PSALM 27:4 NKJV

Evening

We've all been in conversations when the person we're talking with is distracted, looking at their phone and not truly engaging with us, when we don't feel like what we have to say or share is a priority. And we've all been in conversations when the opposite was true, when someone was attentively listening and interested in our time together, when their attention made us feel loved and considered.

We understand it is good and loving to be intentionally present while in the company of others. We should also hold to this when it comes to being present with God, aiming to be purposefully present with Him. When we pray, are we present or just going through the words? When we read the Bible, are we present or just reading the words? When we worship, are we present or just singing the words?

The one thing David desired was to be truly present with the Lord, dwelling with Him and not allowing his gaze to move to anything other than the beauty of the Lord. The experience of God's presence was so rich that it diminished every other desire. May it be the same for us! As we experience God's nearness and companionship, may the desire to continually dwell and commune with Him deepen and grow all the more. For one thing is to be desired, as one thing is necessary.

We read in Luke 10 about Martha and Mary, two sisters who were friends of Jesus and welcomed Him into their home. Martha became "distracted with much serving" (v. 40) while Mary sat at the Lord's feet to listen to His teaching. Although Martha's serving was good and considerate, she became distracted from Jesus. In her anxiety about all that had to be done, she asked that Jesus instruct Mary to help her.

Jesus lovingly reminded Martha of what mattered most: "Martha, Martha, you are anxious and troubled about many things, but one thing is necessary. Mary has chosen the good portion, which will not be taken away from her" (Luke 10:41–42).

We give time and attention to what we cherish most. Or at least we should. Distractions easily tempt us away from truly being present with others and with Jesus. We sometimes strive at the expense of what is most valuable to us. What are we striving to achieve or gain at the cost of our communion with God?

Mary, like David, desired one thing. She desired to be at His feet, dwelling with Him and beholding His beauty. Mary's devotion was made apparent in her attention and her posture, in her yearning to learn from Jesus.

We know there is a time and place to serve and to work. But there are also times when Jesus is calling us to Himself to rest, to learn, to sit at His feet. Take time this morning to pause and consider the beauty of the Lord. You can reflect on the beauty of His heart and character, on His mercy, justice, righteousness, goodness, love, power, holiness, faithfulness, forgiveness, or any other attribute that comes to mind.

Being present with God causes anxiety to flee. When our minds shift to focus on Him, worry no longer has room to keep us bound up. So take hold of the blessing of spending time with Jesus. Take hold of the one thing.

Lord,

May I, like David and Mary, desire You above every-thing. May I seek You all the days of my life, to dwell with You and delight in Your beauty. May I sit at Your feet to be near You.

I long to be as close to You as one possibly can be while on this earth. I long to remain in constant communion with You. Would You answer this prayer of my heart? Amen.

In the Waiting

Those who wait on the LORD shall renew their strength; they shall mount up with wings like eagles, they shall run and not be weary, they shall walk and not faint.

ISAIAH 40:31 NKJV

Morning

Year after year went by as we waited, prayed, and hoped. Some days were so painful as my husband and I waited to see if it was God's plan for us to have a child. The unknown brought such sorrow and weariness at times.

Some seasons of waiting are accompanied by pain and heartache. My heart broke with every negative pregnancy test and every Mother's Day that passed without a baby in my arms. Yet in this season, there was a sweetness that I never would have expected. As I waited, I experienced a deepening relationship with the Lord, a growing dependency upon Him, a renewing of my strength, a refining of my heart, and a building of my faith. In this time, He was preparing me for His will to be done.

Waiting is not easy, but God does have a plan, and trusting in Him is always worth it. So we wait on His timing, His direction, His guidance, His provision, His doors to open, His doors to close, His sovereign plan in all things. Throughout Scripture, "wait" and "hope" are used interchangeably and frequently show up paired together. This signifies that waiting on Him is hoping in Him.

Waiting on God is not passive; it's continually going to Him in prayer, seeking Him and pursuing His heart. It's reading His Word and asking for His guidance as we make decisions within the waiting. And while we wait, He teaches us, transforms us, dwells with us. Perhaps the waiting season itself is a most precious gift of God.

It was ten years my husband and I waited upon the Lord: seven years of infertility and three years in the adoption process. And in His will and timing, He gifted us a beautiful baby girl through adoption! I wrote this morning's prayer while in the season of waiting—a prayer not from the other side but from the middle of the waiting. If you are weary in the waiting today, may you be encouraged by offering these words to the Lord.

Lord,

> *Please strengthen me as I wait, teach me as I wait, transform me as I wait. Despite the moments when waiting*

hurts, Your presence comforts my soul and encourages me to continue to wait on You. And that I will do. I wait for You, my whole being waits (Psalm 130:5).

This time with You is so meaningful because of what happens in the waiting—a deepening relationship with You and a recognition that You remain my joy as I wait. Because no matter what happens, I always have You.

You see the full picture, beginning to end. I do not. And so I put my trust in You. Prepare me for Your will, and may Your will be done. This I know with full certainty: Your timing and plans are good and right and perfect. I love You. In Jesus' name I pray, amen.

I Would Have Lost Heart

I would have lost heart, unless I had believed that I would see the goodness of the LORD in the land of the living. Wait on the LORD; be of good courage, and He shall strengthen your heart; wait, I say, on the LORD!

PSALM 27:13–14 NKJV

Evening

Our season of waiting didn't end when our daughter was born. Although we brought her home from the hospital, our waiting continued for over three months for the adoption to be finalized. Each day that I held my baby girl, I prayed for strength and grace to not guard my heart so I could bond with Norah and love her without the fear of her being taken away. My husband and I prayed fervently for His will for Norah, us, and Norah's wonderful birth mom. God gave me a prayer to pray in this time of waiting: "Help me to love and mother Norah well in whatever time You give me with her."

He again walked me through daily surrender, reframing my focus to trust Him that Norah would be where she needed to be. Whether that meant I would be a mother or not, I knew no matter what, I would always see His goodness. And exactly one hundred days after her birth, we had our finalization court date. It was official! Norah was legally our daughter.

After my mom passed away and before adopting, I would often listen to the song "Goodness of God," crying as I grieved my mama. The lyrics that especially hit my heart were the ones that speak about God leading us through the fire, being near in the darkest nights, and knowing Him as a Father and Friend.[10] Now I listen to this song with Norah all the time, and I realized I have seen the goodness of God in death and in new life, and I am grateful.

Sometimes in our waiting, in our anticipation of something we are longing for, we may become disheartened, which can distort our perception of God's goodness. There may be a temptation to see His goodness only when we are blessed with a desire of our heart, but His goodness is unchanging, no matter the outcome.

He *is* good. Good is His very nature. Our perspective is greatly limited, while His is entirely unlimited. So we trust that He knows best and works all things together for the good of those who love Him (Romans 8:28). His ways are higher than our ways, and His thoughts are higher than our thoughts (Isaiah 55:9). Surrendering to His perspective brings a peace that endures through life's uncertainties.

We read in Lamentations 3, "The LORD is good to those who wait for him, to the soul who seeks him" (v. 25). We see the goodness of God in what He does in the waiting:

He's the God who renews our strength and hope.
He's the God who refines us.

He's the God who reminds us that He never leaves us.
He's the God who refreshes our weary hearts.
He's the God who restores our joy.

Several years ago I woke up one morning with the first word of each of the five prayers below. Then the prayers unfolded over the following days, and they helped give words to my prayers in the waiting. May you also find them helpful in your waiting.

Renew my strength and hope, Lord.
Refine me as I wait, my God.
Remind me I'm not alone in my waiting, Father.
Refresh my weary heart, Jesus.
Restore my joy, Holy Spirit.

Freedom from the
Pressure to Perform

Am I now seeking the approval of man, or of God?
Or am I trying to please man? If I were still trying
to please man, I would not be a servant of Christ.

GALATIANS 1:10

Morning

I sat at the kitchen table and said to myself, "I just can't keep up." I had fallen into a "pressure to perform" trap with creating content on social media, feeling the need to keep providing what I thought was expected of me by others, even though as a new mom I really needed to slow down.

I got up from the kitchen table and went on a walk with my daughter, took a breath, and prayed. My soul was restless, and God showed me why. I felt God in that moment encourage me to stop striving. To lean into what He was calling me to do in this season and let go of the "should dos." I needed to simplify. So I prayed, "God, show me how to simplify." I felt Him guiding me to take a month off social media, to rest and renew my perspective of serving others by following His leading without the pressure to perform on a public platform.

Social media has dramatically increased the desire for approval and the pressure to meet a wholly subjective, ever-changing standard, whether posting is part of your job, your ministry work, or purely for fun. It fuels the need to keep up, keep up the likes, keep providing what people want to see. Instead of looking to God, we turn our attention to being validated by other people's praise. Then when we don't get the recognition or responses we desire, we become dejected and anxious to get back to a place of approval, or we feel like our worth is now somehow less.

Much anxiety comes from living for the approval of others and the pressure to perform. The expectations we place on ourselves for our performance can cause a constant sense of needing to "keep up," which is exhausting and fuels discontentment.

It's an easy trap to fall into, online and in other areas of life: at your job, in your marriage, in your friendships, in your parenting, even in your service. What might start as a desire for others to like you can morph into finding your purpose in the praise of others. Approval, admiration, and kind compliments from people are not bad, but living *for* them is a path to anxiety and discouragement.

We live for the pleasure of God. We live to love God and be loved by God and to do the good works He has entrusted us to do (Ephesians 2:10). We live to serve others, not driven by the desire for their praise or approval but out of our love for them. We live to abide in Christ and for His approval, not man's. When we succumb to the pressure to perform for the approval of others, we don't live from our identity in Christ. We live in the identity people give to us. People can be fickle. God is not. People's praise and love can come and go and are inconsistent, but the love of God remains. Thank God for His steadfast love!

We cannot live simultaneously for both the approval of God and man, because we can't serve two masters. Looking to others for approval takes our eyes off God and costs us our peace, joy, and contentment. The praise and approval of others will never truly satisfy; only Jesus satisfies.

God,

Sometimes I struggle with the pressure to perform and with desiring the approval of others. Sometimes I have fallen for the lie that my worth is determined by the admiration or praises of people. But my value is determined by You. How grateful I am for this truth!

Search my heart and reveal my motives for wanting validation from others. Please forgive me. And please lift off the pressure to perform. Keep me from the temptation to live for the approval of others. My soul knows what an exhausting and dissatisfying place this proves to be.

I don't live for the praise of others; I live to praise You. I love You. In Jesus' name I pray, amen.

God's Beautiful Poem

For we are his workmanship, created in Christ
Jesus for good works, which God prepared
beforehand, that we should walk in them.

EPHESIANS 2:10

Evening

When you hear that you are God's workmanship, what does this mean to you? Do you take to heart the truth of what this means? I didn't fully understand the meaning of the word before looking into it, and when I did, goodness, it moved me. The riches of God's Word are abundant! There is a wealth of meaning in every book, chapter, line, and word.

The *Enduring Word Commentary's* notes on our verse today brought me a deeper understanding and sweeter appreciation for the faithfulness of God. It says, "We are His workmanship, which translates the ancient Greek word *poiema*. The idea is that we are His beautiful poem . . . [a] 'work of art.'"[11]

Take a moment and think about this. You are God's work of art, His beautiful poem. I see God, with great joy, penning His poem of your life. This morning we talked about seeking approval from others instead of from God. How much more should we turn to the God who considers our very lives to be a work of art?

Each word and each line He writes has a purpose and is transforming us more into the likeness of Christ. We do not have to strive or perform for the world; we have peace in being God's poem.

We trust in the Author's ability to bring to completion what He wills for our days, weeks, months, years, and lifetime. Tonight, rest in the assurance that He will help you walk in the good works He has prepared for you.

If you're feeling like you've been struggling with seeking approval from others or living a performance-based life, I want to encourage you tonight:

God has not called you to do all the things.
Pause. Get quiet with God. Pray.
Ask Him to reveal what you need to remove or rearrange or reprioritize.
Ask Him to lead you in what to set your focus and attention on and to give you the peace and courage to let go of the rest. To let go of the "should dos." To let go of seeking approval from others.
Lean into His grace to be present and content in the season He currently has you in, independent of the praise or approval of man.

And know this: "He who began a good work in you will bring it to completion at the day of Jesus Christ" (Philippians 1:6). God is faithful to complete the poem He is writing within you. The world is reading this poem. May it draw others near to Him and may it bring Him all the glory. Day by day, hand Him the pen.

My beloved Poet,

Oh, to be called Your beautiful poem! By Your grace, I am Your workmanship. You are the Author, and I am the work of Your hands.

You intimately write each word, construct each line, are pleased by each stanza. With Your loving attention to detail and intentionality, You spend time working on my heart, making it into a masterpiece. For it is indeed a masterpiece, a work of art, if I look more and more like Jesus.

All the days ordained for me were written in Your book (Psalm 139:16). May I faithfully walk in the good works You have prepared beforehand for me each day. And may these good works give You all the glory. Amen.

"Consider the lilies, how they grow:
they neither toil nor spin."

Luke 12:27

Birds of the Air

"Look at the birds of the air: they neither sow
nor reap nor gather into barns, and yet your heavenly
Father feeds them. Are you not of more value
than they?"

MATTHEW 6:26

Morning

It was June and I was at jury duty, having just been selected as a juror to sit on the panel for a trial. I called my husband on my lunch break to let him know. I could immediately tell something was wrong, then he told me—he had just been laid off. We had experienced stressful financial times before when he had to file bankruptcy because of a business deal falling through, so hearing this immediately brought back feelings of instability. I sat in the car, shocked; we didn't see this coming. But my husband's words brought me to tears and helped me surrender the worries that were quickly surfacing. "We will trust God and trust His plan."

In July, one month later, we were matched to adopt a baby girl after an adoption journey of three years. The timing was interesting, to say the least! Then in August, our precious baby girl was born, and immediately our parenthood journey began.

We began our journey as parents uncertain how we were

going to make it financially. We needed to trust and keep trusting, to depend and keep depending. For eight months, my husband applied and interviewed and prayed until he was hired and began working at a company. But God was working in it all, through family and friends and in miraculous ways. Over and over we saw God providing and stretching what we did have to cover our needs.

This season refined us in our dependence upon God, trusting in His provision and providence in all things. We needed to "look at the birds of the air"—a comforting image to remind us that we would be taken care of and to surrender and rest in our Father's care.

There is a freedom found when we live in the present day with God, not worrying about what is to come but walking one day at a time with Him, keeping our perspective fixed not on worldly or material things but on heavenly things. Peace and contentment come when we cling to God as our Father and believe that He is working all things for good out of His sovereignty, grace, and love.

In this life, you do have needs, needs He already knows before you ask Him (Matthew 6:8). And He is the Meeter of those needs. You are not left on your own, friend. You don't have to live as the world does with the pressure that everything hinges on you. God will take care of you in every possible way, physically and spiritually. I pray you begin your day looking at the birds of the air, reminded of how cherished and cared for you are.

Jesus,

You tell me not to be anxious about my life. You tell me to look at the birds of the air who neither sow nor reap nor gather into barns, and yet the Father feeds them. You tell me I am much more valuable than the birds. You remind me to trust the Father and His care.

And so I exhale and rest in this beautiful promise of the Father's love. I release my worries. I lay down my anxieties. I look at the birds of the air. Amen.

Not Forgotten

"Are not five sparrows sold for two pennies? And
not one of them is forgotten before God. Why, even
the hairs of your head are all numbered. Fear not;
you are of more value than many sparrows."

LUKE 12:6–7

Evening

One afternoon I was sitting in our sunroom when suddenly a bird hit one of the windows. I looked out the window—it was a sparrow. It had fallen to the ground and wasn't moving. My heart dropped. I went outside and started praying to God about the bird. I knew He saw this sparrow fall to the ground; Scripture told me so (Matthew 10:29). After some time had passed, the bird began to move, then jumped to its feet a bit shaken and eventually flew away! I was in tears, not only because I was so relieved and happy that the sparrow was okay, but also because of God's love and consideration for not only the little sparrow but for us, too, as His children.

How kind is our God? He is good to all and has compassion on all He has made (Psalm 145:9). He is all-knowing, all-loving, all-present. To think of Him not forgetting even one sparrow speaks to His intimate awareness of His creation. His eye is on *one* sparrow. If He doesn't forget about one sparrow out of the billion sparrows in this world, then He won't forget you out of the billions of people in this world.

Sometimes in the thick of things, in trials and suffering, I have felt forgotten. I have felt as if relief was delayed. I have felt like my prayers were going unheard while my heart cried out, *Where are You, God?* It is painful to feel forgotten by God. And in those moments, what do we do?

For me, I pray and keep praying. I worship. I seek God's comfort and nearness. I tell Him how much I need Him. I recall scriptures that speak the truth of His character. I remind myself how He has been there for me and with me all my life. And I remember His love. Sometimes we forget how loved we are by Him, how treasured we are. And not only do these verses tell us this, but the crucifixion and sacrifice of Jesus on the cross tell us that we have never been forgotten nor could ever be forgotten. The cross is the ultimate example of the lesson we learn in the sparrow, the ultimate testament of His compassion and mercy.

Jesus reveals to us in tonight's scripture that even the hairs of your head are numbered. If He knows how many hairs you have, He knows the very details of who you are. He knows everything about you, physically, emotionally, mentally, and spiritually. He knows when you feel lonely or forgotten; He knows the extent of your pain and worries. But He never leaves you; He could never forget you, friend. His eye remains on you. His hand remains on you. His love remains on you.

God,

 To consider how You care even for the smallest of Your creations, for a single sparrow, reveals much about Your character. Not one of them is forgotten by You.

 But Father, at times I have felt forgotten. And it hurts to feel this way. You remind me that in those moments, You were there, You saw me. For if You remember the sparrow, You remember me. Because Jesus says I am of more value than many sparrows.

 When I struggle to feel remembered, strengthen my heart to believe the truth that I am not forgotten. Your compassion is evident over all Your creation, it is evident throughout the course of my life, and it is evident in Christ. Amen.

Jesu Juva

The LORD is my strength and my shield; my heart trusts in him, and he helps me. My heart leaps for joy, and with my song I praise him.

PSALM 28:7 NIV

Morning

Johann Sebastian Bach (1685–1750), known as one of the greatest composers of all time, began his compositions by writing the letters J.J. at the top. J.J. is the abbreviation for the Latin phrase *Jesu Juva*, which means "Jesus help" or "Jesus, help me."[12] This was his prayer for each composition.

How beautiful is this? Bach didn't rely on his tremendous talent alone; he relied on Jesus. He was a surrendered vessel to be used by God to accomplish that which God had created him to do. He was dependent on Jesus to create the music through him. He partnered with Jesus through every step of the composition process.

The older I get and the more I walk with Jesus, the more I realize just how much I need Him in everything I do. Looking to Jesus relieves the pressure we place on ourselves when we move in self-reliance and self-dependency, as if the execution, outcome, and achievement are all up to us. Much of our stress comes from living in this place. We forget to lean on the Lord as our Helper to accomplish what He has entrusted us to do.

Much more is accomplished when we ask Jesus for help. And this may not necessarily mean more in the sense of output but more in the growth of our faith, the refinement of our character, the increase of our peace, the magnification of our joy. Jesus daily gives us the strength to walk in our purpose and to complete what we need to.

Modern society moves so fast and demands so much. It is easy to feel like you're falling behind—unless you keep your eyes fixed on Jesus. He is true to His Word. He will help you in completing whatever He has for you within each day as you follow His leading. You can exhale and lay the rest down at the end of the day, trusting that it can wait until tomorrow.

Before you go about your day today, pray "Jesus, I need Your help again." Begin today, just as Bach began each musical piece, intentionally asking Jesus to help you. And as you begin each task within a day, ask Jesus to help you again. Consider this new day a new composition to write with the Lord, and in His graciousness, He will help you all along the way.

Jesus, help me.

Soli Deo Gloria

Not to us, O LORD, not to us, but to your name give
glory, for the sake of your steadfast love and your
faithfulness!

PSALM 115:1

Evening

As we discussed this morning, Bach would begin his compositions with J.J. And at the end of each composition,
he would write S.D.G. at the bottom. S.D.G. is the abbreviation for the Latin phrase *Soli Deo Gloria*, which means "to the
glory of God alone."[13]

What a purposeful way to honor God, by both seeking His
help as he began to compose and giving Him all the glory as he
finished! Bach was devoted to writing his compositions with
excellence and determination for God's glory, all while knowing his desperate need for Jesus' help. Bach wrote his music
with God and *for* God. May the same be said of us in what we
put our hands, talents, and time to.

While Bach was entrusted to compose masterpieces for
the glory of God, we, too, have been entrusted with kingdom
work that is unique to us and important and pleasing to God.
And we, too, are reliant on God's grace throughout the day to
accomplish this work. Everything we do can be done for His

honor and praise. We give Him glory by doing all things out of our love for Him.

Keeping the focus on God's glory alone is the way to safeguard our hearts from self-glorification. I often ask myself, *Am I doing this for my own glory or God's glory?* Living for His glory is the sweetest, most satisfying, most worthy way to live. And a life lived for His glory imprints upon eternity.

We live for God's glory by the help of the Holy Spirit and by asking for forgiveness if He convicts us of seeking glory for ourselves. In His kindness, He shifts our hearts away from exalting ourselves and back to living for God's glory.

Bach wrote his music not for his own glory but for the glory of God. His goal was not for people to praise him but for people to praise God through his music. How amazing that Bach's music would give glory to God through the centuries! I encourage you to pause and play a song by Bach. Maybe you have a favorite you'd like to play, or you can listen to one of my favorites that I find so peaceful before bed: "Air on the G String," "Jesu, Joy of Man's Desiring," or "Arioso."

Every evening, may you rest knowing all has been done by His grace for His glory. Each new day is like a new composition, so tonight consider how you've finished today's composition. Every day you are composing the music of your life—notes and lines that add up to an offering to God.

And today, like Bach, sign off with these words: "To the glory of God alone!"

Father,

I pray that what I do within a day is pleasing to You, that it gives You glory, and that it brings You joy.

May Your Spirit keep my heart from self-glorification, and may Your Spirit keep my heart beating for Your glory alone.

This life is never for my praise, only for Yours.

Never for my name, always Yours.

Never for my glory, forever Yours.

To You be the glory forever and ever. Amen.

I will praise you, Lord my God, with all my
heart; I will glorify your name forever.
Psalm 86:12 NIV

Trusting the One Who
Calms the Storm

He got up and rebuked the winds and the waves,
and it was completely calm. The men were amazed
and asked, "What kind of man is this? Even the
winds and the waves obey him!"

MATTHEW 8:26–27 NIV

Morning

During our adoption journey, we had an adoption fall through. After a birth mother chose us as the adoptive parents of her twin boys, my husband and I, our two dogs, and a variety of baby items flew to the state where she lived right before her due date in excited anticipation. However, the day after she gave birth, our lawyer reached out with the news: She had changed her mind about adoption. Although she was unable to parent, she instead signed over guardianship to a family member.

We knew the risks going into adoption: This was always a possibility and, of course, the right birth mothers have. My husband was adopted, so he and his family brought a needed perspective through it all. Throughout the adoption process, we prayed for God's will and peace for the birth mothers and families, babies, and ourselves. One of the most difficult parts of our journey was hoping and preparing but trying not to hope too much.

Although my head knew the risks, my heart still broke. I questioned: *Will I ever be a mother?* I remember crying so hard, my mind having to adjust suddenly from preparing to be a mother to accepting that now wasn't the time. We had names picked out, car seats to return, flights to change, and an Airbnb that we had to try to get out of early. We were in a state far from home, far from family and our community. While we were there, it was our twelve-year wedding anniversary and my mom's third birthday since passing away.

But Jesus calmed the storm. In the middle of heartbreak and confusion, I felt a deep peace that didn't make sense. And *exactly* one year later, on our wedding anniversary, we had our first conversation with our daughter's birth mother. Then the next day, on my mother's birthday, she told us that she had chosen us to raise and love her baby girl.

Only God! Only God could have orchestrated such sweet timing. Only He heals and redeems the damage from the storms of life. Only He gives such beauty and clarity after the waves and winds are calmed.

Trusting God is easier when life is easier. It's when the storms come, when the trials come—that is when our trust is tested. The level of trust we have in the Lord isn't revealed until it is tried. So when the storms come, we hold on to Him tightly, trusting in Him to calm the storm and calm our hearts.

This morning I encourage you to listen to the old hymn "How Can I Keep from Singing?"[14]

No storm can shake my inmost calm
While to that Rock I'm clinging;
Since Christ is Lord of heav'n and earth,
How can I keep from singing?

Lord,

I trust in You. And when the storms of life come, I will cling to Your goodness and sovereignty. Your steadfast love embraces me. You hold me in the storm; You won't let go. In my trusting, You build my strength, perseverance, and hope.

I do not lean on my own understanding, for Your understanding far surpasses my own. Some people trust in the things of this world. But with all my heart, I trust in You, the One who calms the storms, who speaks to the winds and the waves and they obey. Amen.

A Mind Stayed on God

You keep him in perfect peace whose mind is stayed
on you, because he trusts in you.

ISAIAH 26:3

Evening

When I was a child, I was in gymnastics for several years. After the floor, the balance beam was my favorite event. I was taught to keep my eyes focused on the end of the beam. This would help me stay centered; otherwise I would lose my balance and either wobble or fall off. It took intentionality to stay focused, and at times I would forget, especially when learning a new, challenging skill.

I find it is the same in life when it comes to trusting God. When we keep our eyes and minds fixed on Him, we are more centered, calm, and graced with stability. It takes intentionality to have a mind stayed on God, which results in being kept in His "perfect peace."

It certainly can feel difficult to imagine perfect peace in our lives in the midst of juggling schedules, kids, work, relationships, and everything in between. And then with all the distractions that come in a day, it can be challenging to have a mind "stayed on" God. Yet Scripture tells us that's the source of perfect peace. But what does it actually mean to have a mind stayed on God?

It means to set our gaze and fix our thoughts on Him, to look to Him continuously, to focus on His character and trustworthiness. It's a mind stayed and resting on His glory, His beauty, His kingdom, His faithfulness. When our minds dwell on Him, He keeps us in His complete peace, a peace that weaves through the tapestry of life, that flows through the hills and the valleys.

With our minds, we think on His attributes, meditate on Scripture, and reflect on who God is. With our minds, we recognize and understand that God is in control, He is sovereign, He rules and reigns, and everything is in His hands. We set our minds on the truth, power, excellence, and loveliness of God.

To keep our minds on God, we pray throughout the day and spend time in His Word. We ask the Spirit to direct our thoughts to stay on God because our minds inevitably wander. We talk about God in our conversations, and we pray with one another. We gather in community to learn and worship together at church, and we encourage each other to keep looking to God, especially when challenges come. It's also important we pay attention to the things that may be distracting us and drawing our eyes away from God.

Tonight, before falling asleep, consider what might be a frequent source of distraction from focusing on God. Are there things that your mind is staying on more than God? What is one thing you can do to help your mind stay more on God?

A heart at rest is a heart that trusts. We often long for rest, and that longing is satisfied when we trust God, because rest and trust are connected. We deeply rest when we deeply trust. I pray God would bless you with His perfect peace tonight and that He would help you rest your mind and heart upon Him, always and forever.

God,

Your Word says that You keep those in perfect peace whose mind is stayed on You, because they trust in You. Please show me the things my mind is staying on more than You. O Lord, help my mind stay fixed on You. This is my heart's desire, and I need the help of Your Spirit to keep my thoughts set on You.

May I steady the gaze of my heart on Your holiness, goodness, and love. Guard me from dwelling on worries and lesser things that distract me from You, my perfect peace.

I lie down tonight depending on You with all my heart and with all my mind. In Jesus' name I pray, amen.

In the morning, Lᴏʀᴅ, you hear my voice; in the morning
I lay my requests before you and wait expectantly.

Psalm 5:3 ɴɪᴠ

A Rhythm of Prayer

My heart has heard you say, "Come and talk with
me." And my heart responds, "LORD, I am coming."
PSALM 27:8 NLT

Morning

God has gifted us language to come and talk with Him.
Words and thoughts to share with our gracious Creator.
Prayer is our heart communicating with the Lord, praising
Him for who He is, confessing our sins and our regrets, and
voicing our deepest needs. In prayer, we share with Him vul-
nerably, respectfully, and lovingly.

There is a rhythm of prayer that builds as we pray to Him
daily and continuously. A consistent prayer life is what cultivates a greater closeness to God, so we must make prayer one
of our greatest priorities and greatest joys. This morning, know
He hears your voice as you lay your requests before Him and
wait expectantly (Psalm 5:3). And all throughout your day, you
can and should talk with Him! Because prayer is precious not
only to us but also to God.

As we move in this habitual rhythm of prayer, we are more
inclined to be persistent in coming to God in the midst of our
trials and distress. When the answer hasn't come yet, we keep

praying. When relief hasn't come yet, we keep praying. His help *will* come.

It may not always be immediate, and it may be tempting to stop praying about a circumstance when we don't feel heard by God. It can hurt to keep praying for trials or difficulties to improve and not see relief within the timing we so desire. I've wept over the health needs of my family. I've begged God to intervene when my husband and I were hoping to have a child. When God tells us to wait, it can feel like silence or as though He's abandoned us. But He is faithful, He has not forgotten, and He is at work to bring all things together for good, even when life feels out of control.

Psalm 86 gives us encouragement to be relentless in our prayers, as David prayed: "Be merciful to me, O Lord, for I cry to You all day long. . . . Give ear, O LORD, to my prayer; and attend to the voice of my supplications. In the day of my trouble I will call upon You, for You will answer me" (v. 3, 6–7 NKJV).

So we persist in our prayers, steadfastly trusting that He hears and will respond according to His will and in alignment with His character and promises. Perhaps He is growing and refining us as we wait upon Him, or perhaps He is revealing something about Himself or strengthening our relationship with Him. We may not know exactly why or what, but we *know* He is doing something good as we wait upon Him in prayer. And we trust that in this rhythm of prayer, He is calming our hearts and imprinting His peace on our souls.

Lord,

This morning I lay my requests before You and wait expectantly. In my complete dependency, I bring my prayers to You continuously and persistently.

You beckon my heart to come talk with You, and it brings the sweetest delight and gratitude. Help me to never ignore this opportunity to continually spend time with You, for You are worthy and You are wonderful. With all my heart, I praise You for the beauty of prayer.

May I choose to turn to You in a steady rhythm of prayer throughout my day—morning, evening, and each moment in between. I love You, amen.

A Rhythm of Repentance

Create in me a clean heart, O God, and renew a
right spirit within me.

PSALM 51:10

Evening

There is another rhythm of prayer that is imperative to our
Christian life, and that is one of repentance. The maturing
of our character, the strengthening of our faith, the increased
desire to become more like Jesus are fruit that grows as we
seek God, admit our sins, and with sincere remorse take action
to turn away from them.

When we first repented and believed in Jesus, He took
our sins and forgave us. He gave us a new life and a new
heart. Yet though we receive salvation, we still struggle with
sin (1 John 1:8) and need God's continual help to transform
and sanctify us.

Pastor Tim Keller explains sin in a profound way:

What makes [sin] wrong is not just that I broke a rule, but
I broke His heart; not that I just trampled on His law, but
I trampled on Him; not just I need to repent in order to
get what I want, but I need to repent, otherwise I'm tram-
pling on the very loveliness of God. . . . I have trampled

on a good friend, someone whose love is unfailing, someone whose compassion is infinite.[15]

Therefore, we see the continual need for confession and repentance as part of a relationship with Jesus. In confession, He continues to change us, forgive our sins, and shower us with the mercy and grace we so desperately need. The good news is that "if we confess our sins, he is faithful and just to forgive us our sins and to cleanse us from all unrighteousness" (1 John 1:9). A contrite, repentant heart God will not reject (Psalm 51:17), for He delights to show us mercy (Micah 7:18).

Holding on to unrepented sin can lead to anxiousness, lack of peace, and a heaviness of the soul. Sometimes our hearts feel unsettled because the Spirit is bringing up something we need to confess. We may have been making choices or falling into habits that are harmful to us and offensive to God. It's out of God's holiness, justice, and deep love for us that He instructs us not to sin. Not until I had tasted the true pleasure, goodness, and freedom of a life in Christ could I see my sin for what it truly was: destructive, dark, and devastating. This is the great deception of the world—that sin is pleasurable, good, and brings freedom. But sin enslaves. And it keeps us from finding true freedom in Christ.

I included a guided prayer for tonight so you can take time praying and allowing the Holy Spirit to lead you in confession. Friend, remember that as you go to Him, He meets you with His mercy and readiness to forgive. There is such healing and lightness on the other side.

God,

> Search my heart and reveal my sin.

Spend quiet time with God, listening to the Spirit. Is there anything you need to confess? Is there anything you need to repent and turn away from? Share those things with God.

> I come to You to confess and repent, not out of fear of punishment or consequences but because I love You. I mourn my sin because I have sinned against You, a holy, loving, and great God.

Spend time dwelling on His grace, His forgiveness, and His mercy.

> Thank You for meeting me with compassion and forgiveness. In Jesus' name I pray, amen.

Morning Light

The path of the righteous is like the light of dawn,
which shines brighter and brighter until full day.

PROVERBS 4:18

Morning

As the dawn of a new day brings the joy of new light, I hope you woke up this morning feeling the joy of the lightness found in God's forgiveness. And I hope you feel greater peace knowing Jesus keeps you on the path of righteousness that shines brighter and brighter.

When we confess our sins, His Word promises: "For as high as the heavens are above the earth, so great is his love for those who fear him; as far as the east is from the west, so far has he removed our transgressions from us" (Psalm 103:11–12 NIV). Praise God for His great love and complete and total removal of our sins!

As hard as it can be sometimes to confess and repent, once you bring your sins into the light and lay them before God, the burden of your sin is lifted. Your sin has been removed and cast into the depths of the sea (Micah 7:19) by the power of God's compassion. The darkest night gives way to the morning light. It's like breathing in the cool, crisp morning air when you step outside on a fall day. There's a refreshing and a peace brought to your soul.

As I hope you are discovering, joy is found in His forgiveness; peace is ushered in by His abundant grace. Confession and repentance bring us closer to God and settle our hearts, knowing we can take it all to God and we have been forgiven. It's a daily rhythm and abiding fellowship with the Holy Spirit as we pay attention to His prompting to recognize our sins and heed the conviction He brings to our hearts. And in His goodness and kindness, He helps and strengthens us to continue turning from our sins as we find freedom, lightness, and peace in the radiance of His mercy.

We can rejoice with the psalmist and say, "Come and hear, all you who fear God, and I will tell what he has done for my soul. I cried to him with my mouth, and high praise was on my tongue. If I had cherished iniquity in my heart, the Lord would not have listened. But truly God has listened; he has attended to the voice of my prayer" (Psalm 66:16–19).

Lord,

You are holy and righteous, gracious and forgiving. I delight in Your abounding mercy! I delight in who You are. You are my God, the God of compassion and redemption.

I am so thankful for Your kindness that leads me to repentance (Romans 2:4). I'm so thankful You care deeply about the health of my soul and that You heal me of my sins.

Please move me in a continual rhythm of repentance so that the words of my mouth and meditations of my heart would be pleasing in Your sight (Psalm 19:14). In Jesus' name I pray, amen.

Tucked in God's Grace

Let us then with confidence draw near to the throne
of grace, that we may receive mercy and find grace
to help in time of need.

HEBREWS 4:16

Evening

The throne of grace—what a magnificent descriptor of God's throne and reflection of His gracious character. The One who sits on the throne calls us to Himself as a Father and wraps us in His grace.

Grace is undeserved favor. We don't have to work for His favor; we can't earn grace. It is a gift from God (Romans 3:24). It's God's blessing and kindness upon us not because of anything we have done but purely out of His love and nature. The entire Bible points to God's grace. It is evident throughout every page, beginning to end.

We see God's grace in the forgiveness of our sins and also in our times of need: in His provision and protection, comfort and counsel, support and strength. We can, with confidence, draw near to His throne of grace as His children, seeking Him in our weakness and the trials of life.

One evening as I was sitting in my mama's living room

in Texas, I looked out at the most beautiful sunset, feeling weak and sad. A year prior, my husband and I had moved to California, and this was during one of my many trips to Texas to be her caretaker during her cancer treatments. In that moment, looking at the sunset, I felt God speak to my heart: "My grace is sufficient" (2 Corinthians 12:9). He saw me and, in His kindness, encouraged me with a promise from His Word. Shortly after, I was talking with my sister on the phone, and she mentioned God brought this verse to her mind also. She and I had been alternating flying out to care for our mom, and she, too, was feeling weak and sad. I was in awe of His incredible grace in speaking this message to us both at a time we so needed it!

Grace signifies His love, sympathy, and care for us. He sees us, and He knows our needs, our suffering, our weaknesses. He is witness to it all and pours out His grace, sufficient to carry us and strengthen us, blessing us with the courage and endurance to continue despite our trials. His grace tells us that He is near and has never left us, and He never will.

Like children who feel loved and safe when they are tucked in at night, we, too, as children of God very much need to be reminded that we are loved, cared for, and safe in the arms of our Father before falling asleep. We are tucked in God's grace as we lie down to rest, blanketed in His favor and nestled in His kindness. May you go to bed remembering you are tucked in God's grace tonight and every night.

Gracious God,

I am in awe of Your splendor and filled with gratitude that Your favor is freely given. It's not given based on my merit but solely on Your character and goodness.

By Your grace, I am helped in my time of need. Your grace is sufficient; Your grace is magnified in my weakness. Your grace overflows into every facet of my life and every moment of every day.

I rest in Your grace as You tuck me in tonight. I love You, Father. Amen.

In peace I will lie down and sleep, for you alone, LORD, make me dwell in safety.

Psalm 4:8 NIV

Not Alone

Turn to me and be gracious to me, for I am lonely
and afflicted. Relieve the troubles of my heart and
free me from my anguish.

PSALM 25:16–17 NIV

Morning

In my new season of motherhood, there were moments when I felt alone, especially in the early months with lack of sleep and lack of experience. I often felt like I had no idea what I was doing or how to take care of a newborn. I remember standing at the kitchen sink cleaning bottles, crying as I tried to learn this new role while fighting feelings of inadequacy.

Although my husband was on this journey with me, I still felt alone at times with my own personal struggles in being a new mother. People cannot always understand the depths of our unique experiences or be with us constantly. They are not able to fill a role only God can fill in our lives. Only He is our constant Companion.

It's painful when we feel alone in our suffering, worries, or difficult experiences. Though we feel lonely at times, we are never truly alone. Scripture encourages us that God will never leave us or forsake us (Deuteronomy 31:8). He is our ever-present help (Psalm 46:1) and the One who watches over our coming and going now and forever (Psalm 121:8). The Lord is always with us; He is right beside us (Psalm 16:8).

We can and should be honest with God when we're feeling lonely. In this morning's verses in Psalm 25, David was humbly honest with God. He said, "Turn to me," a plea that shows his and God's closeness, as if to say, "Look at me." The NKJV translates this phrase as "Turn Yourself to me." In David's distress, he knew God's presence was the remedy for his loneliness and would soothe his sorrow. David was no stranger to feeling lonely, but he knew what he needed was the nearness and companionship of God.

Paul shared a similar sentiment in 2 Timothy 4. Paul wrote 2 Timothy, his final letter, from prison in Rome shortly before his death. In chapter 4, he shared how no friend or fellow Christian stood by him at his first hearing or court trial during his Roman imprisonment. Although he was abandoned by others, Paul knew he was not abandoned by Jesus: "At my first defense no one came to stand by me, but all deserted me. May it not be charged against them! But the Lord stood by me and strengthened me" (vv. 16–17).

David asked God to turn to him. Paul said that the Lord stood by him. Both examples describe God's response as physical and personal, indicating the tangible and real relationship they both had with the Lord. One that we, too, can seek to have with Him.

No one can be as close or consistently near as the Lord. He knows you and loves you; you are not alone. As you begin your day, talk with your closest Companion, the One who will walk you through every hour.

Lord,

When I feel lonely, please turn to me and be gracious to me. Please show me that I am not alone, that You are not far away but are right beside me (Psalm 16:8).

Relieve me, Lord, from my loneliness, afflictions, and the troubles of my heart. Come near, Lord. I am like a child contented by a loving parent when You turn toward me.

I cling to Your promise that You are with me always, to the very end (Matthew 28:20). Amen.

Your Comforting Companion

"I will ask the Father, and he will give you another
Helper, to be with you forever, even the Spirit of
truth, whom the world cannot receive, because it
neither sees him nor knows him. You know him,
for he dwells with you and will be in you."

JOHN 14:16–17

Evening

During the Last Supper, Jesus promised His disciples another Helper and Companion: the Holy Spirit. Although Jesus would soon leave physically, fulfilling His earthly ministry, they would never be alone. He would spiritually be with them always, "to the end of the age" (Matthew 28:20), and the Spirit would come to reside in them permanently.

The Holy Spirit is a precious gift who has also been given to us by the Father at the request of Jesus, a beautiful display of the Father, Son, and Holy Spirit interacting on behalf of those in Christ. He dwells in us permanently; we are never without His wonderful companionship. When you feel lonely or alone in your struggles or experiences, you are not left companionless, for the Holy Spirit is *with* you and *in* you. He is your Advocate, Encourager, Comforter, and Counselor. And He is promised to be with us forever. What security and consolation this brings!

He is holy and powerful, and He delights to commune with us. He supports, strengthens, and guides us along the narrow path. We walk with the Spirit in intimate fellowship, dependency, and love. He is attentive to our pain and weakness. He is not only aware but is moved to intercede "for us with groanings too deep for words" (Romans 8:26). We are never alone in our prayers either, as the Holy Spirit helps us pray. And in times of weakness, when we don't know what to pray and words fail us, the Holy Spirit understands what we need and intercedes for us according to the will of God (Romans 8:27).

Later in John 14, Jesus again reassured His disciples of the coming Holy Spirit (v. 26). This verse leads right into the promise of Jesus' peace and encouragement to not let our hearts be troubled (v. 27). The Spirit is deeply connected to this promise and our ability to have untroubled hearts in this world.

Tonight, reflect on the ways you noticed God's presence today as He walked you through every hour. And as you fall asleep, rest in the deep comfort and encouragement of His Spirit. May you continue to grow in your fellowship with the Holy Spirit, and may it be a blessed, treasured relationship.

Holy Spirit, my comforting Companion,

Tonight, I dwell on the richness and beauty of communing with You, on the strength and sweetness that Your companionship brings.

Loneliness dissolves in Your abiding presence, and I ask that You increase my awareness of how very close You are. May I feel Your nearness in greater measure.

Thank You for teaching me and guiding me. Thank You for consoling me in my weakness. When I don't know what to pray for as I ought, I lean on You. I'm so thankful You are with me in all that I experience and that You intercede on my behalf.

I am at peace tonight, knowing that You dwell with me and in me. In Jesus' name, amen.

Stopping to Smell the Roses

Every good and perfect gift is from above, coming
down from the Father of the heavenly lights, who
does not change like shifting shadows.

JAMES 1:17 NIV

Morning

There is something to the old saying, "Stop and smell the roses." It's a reminder to slow down, breathe, and notice God's many blessings. Often in this fast-paced life, we become too busy to stop and savor God and His gifts.

All blessings are within Him and come from Him. And the greatest blessing He bestows upon us is the blessing of Himself. The more we realize this truth in our lives, the more we desire deeper companionship with Him, deeper revelation of His heart, and deeper knowledge of His character. We yearn for more moments of tasting and seeing His goodness (Psalm 34:8). When we walk with Him and commune with Him, we begin to see Him everywhere and in everything. In our Greatest Blessing lie thousands of blessings.

This life is one of discovering His good and perfect gifts every day: in delicious food, close friends, an impactful book, a heartfelt movie, a good cup of coffee, family, pets, hobbies, work, rest, a refreshing walk, a fun board game, a beautiful song, a warm bath, a cup of hot chocolate on a winter night, a rainy day, a sea of sunflowers, a field of tulips, a rose garden, and so on. We delight in Him when we delight in His blessings.

We are blessed in the physical sense and also the spiritual sense to taste and see His goodness. Every good and perfect gift is from the Father (James 1:17), who has also "blessed us in Christ with every spiritual blessing" (Ephesians 1:3). Oh, the abundant spiritual blessings seen in our redemption and adoption as His daughters; the blessings of His grace, wisdom, protection, and comfort; the blessings from the indwelling of the Holy Spirit; the blessing of His peace that surpasses understanding; the blessing of an untroubled heart.

There is such a rich life to experience when we commune with God not only in our quiet times but in all things, in all moments, throughout the day. Thousands of blessings within thousands of moments shared with Him. Don't miss the chance to "stop and smell the roses" today, friend!

God, my Greatest Blessing of all,
    Help me to stop and smell the roses with You today. I
don't want to miss out on tasting and seeing Your goodness.
    As I commune with You, thousands upon thousands of

blessings unfold, blessings beyond my ability to count. How grateful I am for Your gifts and the enduring, priceless blessings in Christ.

No blessing is fully enjoyable without enjoying it with You and recognizing Your goodness in each one. As I experience fellowship with You, I long for it in even greater measure and frequency. Would You bless me, Lord, by deepening my relationship with You? May I grow even closer to You. For my greatest blessing is You.

I love You. In Jesus' name I pray, amen.

Resting in Gratitude

Let them thank the LORD for his steadfast love, for
his wondrous works to the children of man! For he
satisfies the longing soul, and the hungry soul he
fills with good things.

PSALM 107:8–9

Evening

There are thousands of opportunities to give thanks to God
as we intentionally take notice of His blessings within a
day, a month, a year, a lifetime.

It is good to give thanks to the Lord because He is deserving and worthy! Giving thanks demonstrates our love and reverence for Him and keeps us from taking Him or His blessings for granted. Offering thanksgiving brings healing, joy, and peace to our hearts; it strengthens our faith, increases our contentment, fortifies our hope, builds our character, and guards us from coveting. When we find gratitude in God and in His presence and blessings, the allure and temptation of chasing worldly things fades.

In tonight's verses we read, "He satisfies the longing soul, and the hungry soul He fills with good things." It is God who truly and eternally satisfies. Physically and spiritually, He fulfills our needs and deepest longings. The hungry soul is hungry for the good things only God can provide, and underneath this hunger is a hunger for more of God Himself. As we long for deeper companionship with Him, we can be assured that He hears and fulfills this longing. Friend, may we hunger and thirst for more of Him, for we will be satisfied! And may we remain grateful, for our gratitude contributes to the intimacy shared with Him. Delighting in Him and His blessings cultivates a tender, sweet fellowship and joy shared together. What blessings He gives to those who earnestly seek Him (Hebrews 11:6)!

As you lie down to sleep tonight, begin to share with the Lord all that you are thankful for. Start with blessings you noticed within today and then move to blessings within this month, year, season of life, and any other blessings that come to mind. Gratitude makes the heart glad and is the sweetest way to fall asleep.

Lord,

 As I recount Your many blessings, I give thanks to You with my whole heart.

 Your blessings are too numerous to fully count, but still, Lord, I pray to recognize more and more of them, that

I might dwell longer in the posture of gratitude. They say "a picture is worth a thousand words," and I pray that I would have a heart reflective of a thousand thank Yous.

It is You who satisfies, now and for all of eternity! Thank You for the good things You fill my soul with; thank You that You satisfy my deepest longing with Your presence.

Thank You for the blessing of sharing another day with You. Amen.

May the God of hope fill you with all joy and peace
as you trust in him, so that you may overflow with
hope by the power of the Holy Spirit.

Romans 15:13 NIV

Where Morning Dawns

The whole earth is filled with awe at your wonders;
where morning dawns, where evening fades, you
call forth songs of joy.

PSALM 65:8 NIV

Morning

He is the God who suspends the earth over nothing (Job 26:7), who laid the foundations of the earth and determined its dimensions, who keeps the sea inside its boundaries, who directs the movement of the stars, who knows the laws of the universe and uses them to regulate the earth, who is wise enough to count all the clouds, who commands the morning to appear, causing the dawn to rise in the east (Job 38). This is the God we hope in and find our joy in.

As morning dawns, hope dawns. Each day, hope sweetly greets us, yet sometimes we miss its greeting, and hope gets drowned out by our worries. But God has graced us with a better way. Our hope is not like the hope of the world. It does not change with seasons or with public opinion. Our hope is "an anchor for the soul, firm and secure" (Hebrews 6:19 NIV). The hope we have in Christ has the power to silence our worries. But we must take hold of this anchor and use it daily.

Biblical hope is a hope that is certain, a hope set on God's faithfulness and sovereignty, a hope built on Christ. Ours is a hope that trusts in God throughout all of life's conditions and one that remains confident in God's promises. When we hope in His help, we can confidently anticipate Him being our help. When we hope in His strength, we can confidently anticipate Him being our strength. And when we hope in His peace, we can confidently anticipate Him being our peace.

Every morning is a new day to eagerly remind your heart to hope in Him again today! For His goodness and faithfulness met you yesterday and will meet you again today. His glory and greatness proclaimed at the dawning of the day give us fresh confidence to hope in Him.

As morning dawns, joy dawns. Oh, how a sunrise scatters joy across an awakening sky. The One who daily crafts a sunrise is our daily joy. "Splendor and majesty are before him; strength and joy are in his dwelling place" (1 Chronicles 16:27 NIV). Our highest privilege and our greatest joy are to commune with Him and to meet with Him as the morning dawns.

When we focus on our worries more than God, our hearts drift into discouragement and despondency. We are communing with our worries rather than with God; we are communing with anxiety rather than the Almighty. As we confess and surrender our cares to Him, in His tender love He draws us to Himself, reminding us that our hope and joy are found in Him.

The scripture below is my prayer for you today. I invite you to read it aloud, imagining a friend praying this over you:

"May the God of hope fill you with all joy and peace as you trust in him, so that you may overflow with hope by the power of the Holy Spirit" (Romans 15:13 *NIV*). Amen.

Where Evening Fades

On my bed I remember you; I think of you through
the watches of the night. Because you are my help, I
sing in the shadow of your wings.

PSALM 63:6–7 NIV

Evening

Joy can look different at various times and in various seasons. Some seasons are heavier with sorrow and some
lighter with joy, and then there are seasons when you feel you're
holding both simultaneously. I experienced this firsthand when
I held my daughter for the first time, thanking God for the
blessing of motherhood while mourning the loss of my own
mother.

Nature illustrated this point to me about two years after
my mom passed away. I was at my favorite gardens, and it had
just rained. I remember stopping to look at some beautiful
azaleas (one of my mom's favorite flowers). Raindrops were
sprinkled on their bright pink petals. *What a contrast*, I thought.
It symbolized to me that joy and tears can coexist in this life,
and often do.

Christian joy is not a forced or fake joy. It is not a joy that
disregards sorrow or suffering. Our tears and moments of sadness do not indicate our lack of joy in the Lord or lack of faith

in Him. If our joy is found in Christ, and He is who we run to, our joy remains even in the middle of tears because our joy *is* Him. And in faith we are trusting Him to be our God, the joy of our life.

I love this metaphor from John Piper on Christian joy:

> There are waves of sorrow and pain and loss that break, big waves that break, over the unshakable rock of Christian joy, and these waves submerge the laughter in the surging. You can feel it: the surging surf of weeping that wells up unbidden from your heart. But they don't dislodge the rock, and the waves recede in due time, and the rock glistens again in tearless sunlight.[16]

Our joy remains because we have a hope that's not rooted in this world. We may be sorrowful yet still rejoicing (2 Corinthians 6:10). And we rejoice that even in the middle of our suffering, more hope is being produced (Romans 5:3–5).

God, the source of our hope and joy, paints every evening sky. When we stop to delight in His greatness and artistry, hopelessness and discouragement fade. And we know that tomorrow, as morning dawns, hope and joy will dawn again.

God, joy of my life,

In peace, I will lie down and sleep tonight, for You are my safe place, my hope, and my joy. When sorrows come, I take comfort in the shadow of Your wings. And by Your grace, joy is still found inside the suffering.

Please continue to renew and strengthen my hope daily. And may the fruit of joy flourish within me by the power of the Holy Spirit.

As morning dawns and evening fades, I see Your glory and faithfulness, and my heart worships You. I love You. Amen.

The LORD will guide you always; he will satisfy your
needs in a sun-scorched land and will strengthen
your frame. You will be like a well-watered
garden, like a spring whose waters never fail.
Isaiah 58:11 NIV

A Heart Like a Garden

"Blessed are the pure in heart, for they shall see God."

MATTHEW 5:8

Morning

Roses, irises, dahlias, lilies, tulips in shades of blue, white, purple, pink, and yellow. Each flower rooted in Christ, each bloom reflective of all the times we have sought God, trusted Him, and loved Him. Through the rain and sun, winter and spring, through every season, we have been learning what it means to cultivate an untroubled heart, a heart like a garden.

It is a garden that endures, grown by tending to our relationship with God. It is a garden we intentionally and lovingly nurture, day by day, where we plant seeds, sowing with the Spirit, and water the garden with "rivers of living water" (John 7:38) that continually cleanse our hearts. Where the righteousness of Christ rains, growing flowers of righteousness; where His light daily dawns, bringing warmth and joy. We submit to His pruning to maintain the health, growth, and integrity of the garden. We clear away the weeds and till the soil, making space for the garden to flourish. We marvel at the blooming of the flowers, overflowing with thankfulness that it is together with Him we are cultivating this garden within our hearts.

The condition of our hearts is deeply significant to God. Scripture tells us that "man looks on the outward appearance, but the LORD looks on the heart" (1 Samuel 16:7). Those who have "clean hands and a pure heart" (Psalm 24:4) are those with an honest and undivided heart, a heart that only worships God, one that loves Him with full devotion. The pure in heart are blessed to see God. And when our eyes look upon Him, our hearts are calmed and untroubled.

It is only by His mercy and the Holy Spirit that our hearts are purified; it is only by time spent with Him and His Word that our hearts are transformed. This is the firm foundation to a thriving relationship with God, just as rich soil is key to a thriving garden. We read in the parable of the sower how important the condition of the soil is when Jesus said, "As for [the seed] in the good soil, they are those who, hearing the word, hold it fast in an honest and good heart" (Luke 8:15). The condition of the soil reflects the condition of the heart. When we sow seeds of goodness and righteousness in sanctified soil with an honest and sincere heart, we will reap a heart like a garden.

Every act of hope, every act of love, every act of faith is planting, watering, and growing the garden in your heart as you abide in Christ. Every flower displays the goodness and majesty of God. Every flower gathers into a garden of faith, a garden that has endured and will endure, by His grace, until our last breath and for all eternity.

Father,

Oh, that I would have a pure heart! Honest, faithful, and true to You. My heart is purified as I cultivate my relationship with You and as we tend to the garden of my heart alongside one another.

Every rose pruned to give You honor, every iris culti-vated to give You glory, every dahlia planted to give You delight, every lily watered to give You worship, every tulip nurtured to give You praise, every flower cared for to give You love.

When my days here are done, may this be an offering to You. When I come to heaven, I pray to bring the garden of my heart to You, that it would be pleasing to You. To hand You my heart that we have grown together. Amen.

To Know Him Is to Love Him

"You shall love the Lord your God with all your heart and with all your soul and with all your strength and with all your mind."

LUKE 10:27

Evening

God desires for us to know Him. Not just intellectually, but also relationally and personally. This invitation to know Him in this way speaks volumes of who He really is and the tenderness and depth of His heart.

In Jeremiah 9 God says, "Let not the wise man boast in his wisdom, let not the mighty man boast in his might, let not the rich man boast in his riches, but let him who boasts boast in this, that he understands and knows me, that I am the LORD who practices steadfast love, justice, and righteousness in the earth. For in these things I delight, declares the LORD" (vv. 23–24). Knowing God is more than intellectually knowing about Him. It is knowing Him in relationship, understanding who He truly is.

Our greatest joy and satisfaction are found in knowing Him. We learn about His character not only in His Word but also by experience. As A. W. Tozer affectionately wrote, "Once the seeking heart finds God in personal experience there will be no further problem about loving Him. To know Him is to love Him and to know Him better is to love Him more."[17] How true I have found this to be! The more I get to know Him through the ups and downs of life, through the trials and joys and daily moments, the more I grow in my love for Him.

We are to love Him with every bit of who we are. We love Him with our emotions and affections, with our understanding, intellect, and thoughts, with our might and ability, with every breath of life in us. And this type of love grows from companionship with Him throughout the moments, days, months, and years of life.

To know Him, we must spend time with Him. And the sweet truth is that He also finds joy in communing with us. A good question we can continually ask God is, "What do You want to reveal about Yourself in this day, in this season, in this circumstance, in this trial, in this blessing?" And in His answers, we get to see and love Him more and more.

So let us take every opportunity to know Him greater, because to personally experience God is the ultimate privilege and happiness of all. Every day, we can walk in close fellowship with Him. Every day, we are making memories with Him, with the aim of seeking Him and living a life that is reflective of our love for Him. And when the goal of our life is to know God more, we will know more peace.

Lord,

I am so grateful for the immeasurable gift of getting to know You greater each day. Each day I pursue You is another day I see Your true nature and goodness. Each day I choose to honor You with my time and attention is another day that nourishes our relationship.

Please bless me by teaching me more about You, for I want to know You better. To know You is my greatest pleasure, to love You is my highest honor. May my love for You be evident in all that I do.

I love You, Lord, with all that I am. My heart is Yours always and forever. Amen.

The name of the LORD is a strong tower;
the righteous run to it and are safe.

Proverbs 18:10 NKJV

The Lord Is My Shepherd

The LORD is my shepherd; I shall not want. He
makes me lie down in green pastures. He leads me
beside still waters.

PSALM 23:1–2

Morning

I n my bedroom I have a much-loved painting hanging above
my dresser. It is of Jesus walking in a field of flowers in all
shades of pink, carrying a lamb across His shoulders. It beautifully illustrates verse 11 in Isaiah 40: "He tends his flock like
a shepherd: He gathers the lambs in his arms and carries them
close to his heart" (NIV).

Calling the Lord our Shepherd speaks of His continual
presence, protection, and provision. A shepherd lives with his
flock and is devoted to their care. A shepherd guides, defends,
and heals his sheep. Jesus referred to Himself as our Good
Shepherd (John 10:11), which reveals so much about His role
in our lives, His compassion and vigilant care as He guides,
protects, and provides for us.

He leads us through the hills and valleys of life, including
the valley of the shadow of death (Psalm 23:4). And although
death can feel like a heavy thought, it is made lighter and glorious when we know who will be right by us, comforting us and
driving away all fear by His presence.

I walked through this valley with my mom, and I can attest to His comfort. He began to prepare my heart that my mom's care needed to shift, from an attempt to bring her cancer into remission to a focus on keeping her as comfortable as possible. God gave me hope in the face of it all. One morning I woke up knowing God wanted me to talk to my mom about hospice care before her doctor's appointment. I remember sitting in her car after running an errand and saying through tears to God, "Okay, I will, but please give me every word to say to her."

I had no idea how to broach the topic of end-of-life care with my mother. I didn't have the words or the strength, but He entirely took over. What I feared would be an impossibly heartbreaking conversation was instead one filled with deep hope, peace, and reverent joy. She was so radiantly calm and cradled in His care. God prepared us both that day before the doctor mentioned hospice to her. Our hearts were already comforted and strengthened as we privately made the decision together first.

He walked us both through this valley, hand in hand with Him and with one another, as He shepherded her toward her final breath. It was a precious, sacred moment, and I thank God He gifted me the honor of being by her side and witnessing Him bringing her home.

We were created to need our Shepherd: "It is he who made us, and we are his; we are his people, the sheep of his pasture" (Psalm 100:3 NIV). As His flock, we are continually under His sovereign care. How refreshing it is to follow His leading beside still waters. How freeing it is to know He will shepherd us through every hill and every valley.

My Good Shepherd,

You are the Guardian of my life. You know what lies ahead, and You lead the way. You gather me in Your arms and carry me close to Your heart.

You are my safe place, my peace, my protection.

Thank You that You are my Shepherd, that You call me by name, and that I know Your voice (John 10:3–4).

In trust, I follow You along still waters. In peace, I lie down in green pastures. Amen.

Under His Wings

He will cover you with his feathers, and under his
wings you will find refuge; his faithfulness will be
your shield and rampart.

PSALM 91:4 NIV

Evening

In Scripture, when we read a reference to being under His
wings, it is a metaphor that points us to His loving care and
protection. Like a mother bird giving refuge to her young from
storms or predators, this image provides another illustration
of His sweet nearness, like the Shepherd who carries us close
to His heart. He draws us under His wings with the deepest
affection.

Under His wings we find safety and security, a break from
the worries and chaos of life, a respite from the busyness of life.
Under His wings we remember we are His children and experience peace not of this world. Under His wings we are hidden
in His love and tender care.

I think of the times I've received a much-needed, comforting hug. That's what I envision when He pulls us under His
wings, where we feel seen and loved by Him, where we feel His
compassion and reassurance that we are not alone, and where
our weariness dissolves in His presence.

How incredible when we consider just how close He really is. And that He desires this closeness too. Scripture tells us, "The LORD is near to all who call on him" (Psalm 145:18). So let us with needful and sincere hearts continue praying, seeking, trusting, and praising Him.

When my mother passed away, I knew that I would be heartbroken at the loss. I knew that I would feel her absence every day until we were reunited in heaven. But what I wasn't prepared for was how utterly and completely loved and protected I would feel as I mourned her passing. The Lord was quick to scoop me up under His wings and keep me close, reminding me that I wasn't abandoned, I wasn't alone, and that even as my mom and dad were now both gone from this earth, I was far from an orphan. I had a Heavenly Father who was ready to love me and protect me, and He made sure I felt that care safely beneath His wings.

I wonder, once we get to heaven, will we know or see just how much He protected us and how many times we were underneath His wings? Will we see how He sheltered us in the storms, how He covered us in the heat of day, how He consoled us in the dark nights?

Tonight, I pray you would feel the comfort of God's love covering you and a confident peace knowing that the Lord Most High is your safe place and refuge. Under His wings you will find rest.

The following are reminders from Scripture of God's protection to read and refer to when needed. As you read through the verses, I hope your heart is calmed and that you tangibly feel the closeness of the Lord, folding His protective wings around you.

Psalm 5:11
Psalm 61:1–4
Psalm 91
Proverbs 18:10
Isaiah 43:2
John 10:28–30
2 Thessalonians 3:3
2 Timothy 4:18

Lord,

Relief washes over me that I am not alone. You are with me. You protect me, You comfort me. Your presence guards me against worries and fears.

My soul is content when I'm near You. You are my Refuge and my Safety, the One I trust with my whole heart.

I rest tonight under the shelter of Your wings, under the protection of Your love. Amen.

Set your minds on things above,
not on earthly things.

Colossians 3:2 NIV

The Scent of Heaven

"Let not your hearts be troubled. Believe in God;
believe also in me. In my Father's house are many
rooms. If it were not so, would I have told you that
I go to prepare a place for you? And if I go and
prepare a place for you, I will come again and will
take you to myself, that where I am you may be also."

JOHN 14:1–3

Morning

Four days before my mama left for heaven, I remember her saying, "I'm ready to go to the Father." As I looked at her, I could see so clearly a peace I cannot explain and a readiness for heaven reflected in her deep blue eyes.

Throughout the year of her cancer journey, my mom would frequently tell us she smelled a wonderful scent of flowers. None of us could ever smell it. Then, on the night she passed away, as the time drew closer to her leaving, all of a sudden my husband got up and began to walk around the room, trying to figure out where a floral fragrance was coming from. The hospice nurse also began to smell it.

At first I didn't smell anything. But then suddenly, I did too! It was like the scent of a garden overflowing with the loveliest blooming flowers, a fresh, soft, yet strong fragrance that you could never tire of smelling. It was the most beautiful smell I've ever smelled, unlike anything I've smelled before. Then, right after she passed, the scent disappeared. I believe in that moment we were all given a cherished glimpse of heaven.

We started day one of our journey in John 14 with Jesus' words to not let our hearts be troubled (v. 27), and we end our last morning encouraged by His words again (vv. 1–3), along with one of the greatest reasons we can have untroubled hearts in this world—our hope in heaven. Two promises we can continually find comfort in: He gives us His peace that's not of this world (v. 27), and He goes to prepare a place for us (vv. 2–3).

In Luke 23:43, when Jesus referred to heaven as a paradise, the Greek word can also refer to a garden. Our hearts are calmed not only by His peace but also His promise of paradise. He has gone to prepare a place for us, a place that is glorious. And while He is preparing a place for us, He is also preparing us for that place. He is at work here, too, turning our hearts from troubled, anxious places into blooming gardens that reflect the perfect paradise we will one day see.

Happiness comes as we contemplate the beauty of heaven, the incredible sights and scents, the love, the holiness, the joy, and, more than anything, dwelling in the full presence of God. This life is one of allowing heavenly things to take root in our own hearts, anticipating paradise while tenderly watering and nourishing our relationship with Him now.

May we abide daily in the joy that Jesus goes to prepare a place for us, where God will wipe away every tear from our eyes and where sin and death will be no more (Revelation 21:4). May our cares fade in the light of our heavenly hope. And as we live in this hope, may we focus on what truly matters: worshiping God; loving Him and loving others; glorifying our Father and praying for His will to be done on earth as it is in heaven; walking with the Spirit and seeking His leading in all things; following Jesus and making Him known; sharing about His love and abiding in His love. In this eternal purpose, we will know a peace from heaven that remains despite trials and a joy that the world can never provide.

The One who prepares a place for me,

Thank You, Jesus, that through You and because of You, heaven is my home. You have planted eternity in my heart (Ecclesiastes 3:11). Oh, how I wait with such anticipation to see Your beauty and glory!

When I become consumed with things that don't matter eternally, please shift my focus to You. Lift my gaze and set my eyes on heaven. For the troubles of this world grow dim when I rest my heart upon You. Amen.

Shalom, Peace

Now may the Lord of peace himself give you peace
at all times in every way.

2 THESSALONIANS 3:16

Evening

The tension we hold as Christians is being citizens of heaven but living currently in this world. We have this longing for heaven, yet we also have this gift of life to be lived here, with all of its beauty, pain, growth, suffering, sanctification, tears, and laughter. And in all of it, we learn more about who God is. We grow in relationship with Jesus and grow more into His likeness. And we are promised His complete and perfect peace, true shalom, as we walk with Him day by day, moment by moment.

Reflect on this journey, these thirty days of starting and ending your day by coming to God to untrouble your heart. His heavenly perspective invites you to embrace His shalom, His true peace, by bringing your burdens to Him and being in constant communion with Him. That constant interaction and desire to be with and confide in God is the way to experience the sustaining peace that can only be found in Him.

As you continue on this path of peace, keep going to Jesus whenever you feel weary or worried. He is always right there to be your help and strength. Keep casting all your cares on Him and releasing all your tears to Him because He cares for you. Each morning, take hold of God's guiding hand, and each night, rest in His fatherly embrace.

When life is good, when life is hard, when you feel joyful, when you feel sorrowful, when you feel victorious, when you feel defeated, you can bring it all to God. When we intentionally keep close to Him, our hearts become untroubled, and we experience peace that surpasses all understanding.

As you live with an eternal perspective, may you continue in the work God has for you here, and may you see the joy and honor of living this life with Him and for Him. May you be filled with peace and purpose as you await with eager anticipation your eternal home. May the Lord bless you and keep you all the days of your life; may He turn His face toward you and give you peace (Numbers 6:24–26). And may the Lord watch over your heart, keeping it untroubled.

Lord,

You are the peace of my life, the joy of my life, the meaning of my life. Being loved by You and knowing You is the blessing above all blessings.

Thank You for walking with me through these thirty days, spending special time with me morning and evening. Please continue growing our relationship and cultivating the garden of my heart, that it would be pleasing to You.

And when worries and difficulties arise, remind me to come quickly to You. Help me to just breathe. In and out, breathing with You, casting my cares on You because You care for me. And keep my heart near Yours, the only place it can remain truly untroubled.

I love You so much. In Jesus' name I pray, amen.

"The LORD bless you and keep you; the LORD make his face shine on you and be gracious to you; the LORD turn his face toward you and give you peace."

Numbers 6:24–26 NIV

Notes

1. "What is the heart?" Got Questions, https://www.gotquestions.org/what-is-the-heart. html.
2. Augustine of Hippo, *Confessions* (Oxford University Press, 1998).
3. Charles Haddon Spurgeon, "The Drawings of Divine Love" (The Spurgeon Center for Biblical Preaching at Midwestern Seminary, *Metropolitan Tabernacle Pulpit*, Volume 40), https://www.spurgeon.org/resource-library/sermons/the-drawings-of-divine-love/#flipbook/.
4. "Glenn: Space adventure 'strengthens my faith,'" CNN.com, November 1, 1998, www. edition.cnn.com/TECH/space/9811/01/shuttle.02/.
5. Tara Carlson, "What Are Moonflowers?" Petal Talk, April 25, 2017, https:// www.1800flowers.com/blog/flower-facts/what-are-moonflowers.
6. John Piper, "God Is Always Doing 10,000 Things in Your Life," Desiring God, January 1, 2013, https://www.desiringgod.org/articles/god-is-always-doing-10000-things-in-your-life.
7. The Discovery Bible, HELPS Lexicon | NASEC Dictionary, https://biblehub.com/greek/1162.htm.
8. Charles Haddon Spurgeon, *The New Park Street Pulpit, Volumes 1–6*, and *The Metropolitan Tabernacle Pulpit, Volumes 7–63* (Pasadena, Texas: Pilgrim Publications, 1990).
9. "Star Basics," NASA, https://science.nasa.gov/universe/stars/.
10. "Goodness of God" by Bethel Music.
11. "Ephesians 2—God's Way of Reconciliation," Enduring Word, https://enduringword. com/bible-commentary/ephesians-2/.
12. "The Life and Faith of Johann Sebastian Bach: 'Soli Deo Gloria'" (To the Glory of God Alone), Christianity.com, December 20, 2022, https://www.christianity.com/wiki/people/j-s-bach-soli-deo-gloria-to-the-glory-of-god-alone-11635057.html?amp=1.
13. Ibid.
14. "How Can I Keep from Singing?" by Robert Lowry, https://library.timelesstruths.org/music/How_Can_I_Keep_from_Singing/.
15. Tim Keller, "Healing of Sin (Part 1)," Gospel in Life, March 24, 1996, https:// gospelinlife.com/sermon/healing-of-sin-part-i/.
16. John Piper, "Does Joy Come After Suffering, or in It?" Desiring God, interview with John Piper, episode 1563, December 18, 2020, https://www.desiringgod.org/interviews/does-joy-come-after-suffering-or-in-it.
17. A. W. Tozer, *The Root of the Righteous* (Chicago: Moody Publishers, 2015).

About the Author

KARA STOUT is a writer, wife, and new adoptive mom living in Los Angeles, California. Kara has written devotionals for Her True Worth, a women's online ministry. Kara has her bachelor's degree in psychology from Arizona State University and her master's degree in counseling from Loyola University Chicago. After walking through a personal medical crisis and the loss of both of her parents to cancer, her life radically changed, and her complete dependency on God for strength and peace became a nonnegotiable. Her hope is to encourage women in their faith, pointing them to their Great Comforter and Greatest Companion.